Hell's Guest

"I grew up in South Alabama in the 1930s. Looking at the world through the cotton and corn fields of Lowndes County, I could never have imagined that in just a few short years the entire world would be engulfed in war and that I would be caught in the middle of it. Where I lived, events in Europe and Asia, as menacing as they were, seemed light years away. I would soon discover that they were not so far away after all . . ."

So begins this powerful memoir by an Alabama boy who ran away to join the army at the age of 16 and six months later found himself in the doomed struggle to save Bataan from the Japanese advance. He was captured, marched north in the infamous Bataan Death March and spent the next three and a half years struggling for his life in Japanese POW camps. Glenn Frazier is an American above all else, one who loves his country and its flag, who catches us all up in his story and teaches the one lesson we all need to learn and relearn: our liberty is our most precious possession and worth the price we must pay to preserve it.

Hell's Guest

This book will help you over came any challenge— May Many blessings come to you and yours—

Col. Glenn Frazier—

www.HellsGuest.com
usafirst2008@yahoo.com

Hell's Guest

Glenn D. Frazier

Manufactured in the United States of America

ISBN 0-9717039-5-7

THIS BOOK IS DEDICATED to all men and women who fought and died in the Philippine Islands during World War II and in the defense of Bataan and Corregidor, and to all those who worked so hard at the time of World War II, be it at home or on the battle fields to save the world from becoming slaves to two world powers that tried to take away our basic right to be free people and to live as God intended us to live with the right to determine our own destiny;

To the men and women who have worn the uniform to serve their country since the formation of the republic;

To my dear friend and working partner on Bataan, Gerald Block, whom the Japanese burned alive at Nichols Field. His personal bravery during the fighting was an inspiration to me and to many other American and Filipino scouts and solders;

To the families that never knew what happened to their loved ones;

To the men and women who never saw our American flag fly again after the Japanese raised the Rising Sun Flag over our dead. May God be with them and never let us forget the cost of freedom paid for with our men's and women's blood that was not shed in vain. Let their sacrifice be a shining light for future generations, and teach them that freedom must be preserved at all costs. No one knows what slavery is all about until he has walked in the shoes of those who have been slaves;

To my family, which suffered long and sorely, waiting to know if I were still alive.

To my cherished friend, Dr. James Strickhausen, who has done so much to support my effort in making this book a reflection of my experiences through a long and difficult time in my life. I give him my special thanks. Without him this book would never have been published;

And to the following people who did so much to make *Hell's Guest* a reality: my wife, Elizabeth Terri Frazier; Dr. Ferrel Killingsworth; Mrs. Frances S. Weiner.

Glenn D. Frazier
Daphne, Alabama 2007

Table of Contents

Foreword

ON APRIL NINTH 1942, General King surrendered Bataan. The Death March started the morning after. Every hundred yards or so there seemed to be a Japanese cameraman taking pictures of us. The one on the cover of this book shows me (third from the left) and my comrade Gerald Block (towel around his neck) early in the march. I was looking for the flagpole that always had Old Glory flying in the breeze. I was devastated that we had had to surrender to the enemy. My spirits were lower than they had ever been before, and I knew that our lives were changing with every step we took.

As we marched down the hill, I looked to my right and glimpsed the Japanese rising sun waving where our flag had been the day before. My heart was broken. I felt numb, and it was hard to keep going. I pointed to the flag pole for Gerald to see. By the look on his face I could tell that he was feeling the same things I was.

Overnight everything had changed. Our freedom had absolutely disappeared. Little did we know that the Japanese would not honor the Geneva Convention rules on how to treat prisoners of war. Everything was gone. We had no constitution to protect us. Americans and Filipinos were being shot or bayoneted to death for trying to get to an artesian well for a drink of water. We had nowhere to turn. Our promised reinforcements had never arrived. We were at the mercy of our captors for everything that might keep us alive

It seems to me that this picture tells the story of our nation today, just played out in a different scenario. Our flag is not honored as it should be. Our justice system is being compromised and is in disarray. There is no protection for the innocent. It is up for sale to the highest bidder.

People with influence make a lie the truth and the truth a lie. Our constitution is being compromised. Our law enforcement officers are seizing private property at will. Our phones are being tapped without a warrant. Some federal courts are being run by the rule of kangaroo courts, guilty before trial. Abraham Lincoln warned, "a house divided against itself, will not stand." Today, our senate and congress are divided as never before. Our freedom is being chipped away a little piece at a time.

Most Americans just sit back and let our elected officials herd us down the wrong road, just as we were herded to our deaths on Bataan. We were shot or bayoneted or taken to starvation. And as we did then, our young men and women are standing in the gap now, without the proper strength to defend themselves.

History does repeat itself. Read this book and put yourself in my shoes and see where this scenario leads. I know the answer because I have lived it myself.

Colonel Glenn Frazier

— 1 —

The Boy I Was

I GREW UP IN SOUTH Alabama in the 1930s. Looking at the world through the cotton and corn fields of Lowndes County, I could never have imagined that in just a few short years the entire world would be engulfed in war and that I would be caught in the middle of it. Where I lived, events in Europe and Asia, as menacing as they were, seemed light years away. I would soon discover that they were not so far away after all. The impact that the war would have on the rest of my life would have been unimaginable to me even if I had foreseen the details of my participation in it: the Japanese attack on the Philippines, the desperate fight for Bataan, the Death March north from the peninsula, and the terrible years struggling for survival in Japanese prisoner of war camps. There was nothing in my experience to measure such things.

My home town was Fort Deposit, population 1500. Small towns in lower Alabama, like so many others in the Deep South, did not have electricity or even running water. Elementary sanitation was relegated to the outhouses that stood at the far limit of every back yard. There was no TV, and even radio programs were often garbled and distorted by static. The icebox was the only way to keep food cool, unless you put the food in a bucket and lowered it into the water at

11

the bottom of the well. Clothes and linens were washed by hand and hung on a line to dry.

We were in the midst of the Great Depression in those years, but my family was better off than most. My father owned a grocery store, and though he was tough on us boys, (there were six of us, three older brothers and two sisters; and myself) he was a generous man who seldom turned anyone away from his counter simply because they could not pay. I remember that after he died in the 1950s, people were still coming by to pay off debts they had made years before. Dad also had a mill that ground the best cornmeal in the county.

My mother was what you might call a pillar of the Methodist Church. Friends would visit on Sunday after services were over. It was the custom that if you invited someone to visit on Sunday, they were expected to come for Sunday dinner. There was lots of food and conversation, and on warm days everyone would sit on the front porch to enjoy every faint breeze and talk, often about the Civil War and World War I, telling and retelling stories about who had gone to serve, what they had done, and who had been killed. Our world seemed to have changed little since those distant events had taken place. Nevertheless, change was on the way.

When the Depression began to wane and the economy began improving, major highways were paved and automobile companies started making fast cars that could take advantage of them. Until that time you were doing good to do thirty or thirty-five miles an hour on the old dirt roads. Then came a Ford with a V-8 engine. Man, what a car! It would run 70 to 80 miles per hour. My Dad bought one—a shiny, black sedan.

Until that time my Dad had never been out of the state of Alabama. His life's ambition was to go to Texas to see an uncle who had moved there using a covered wagon to transport his family and belongings. This uncle had been back to Alabama only once since moving to Texas. Well, around 1936 Dad was able to make that trip—and a lot faster than he had ever thought possible—in an automobile.

By 1939 THINGS WERE changing fast. Country homes were hooking up to the new electric lines. By 1940 most homes had electric refrigerators, inside bathrooms, and running water. When someone got a washing machine, it was the talk of the town. It was a new era and no one was complaining. Just over the horizon, though, there were gathering clouds. What would become the Second World War had begun in Europe. Hitler had overrun Poland, and England and France were under attack. Prime Minister Churchill was doing everything he could to involve America in the war, but President Roosevelt, very much aware of the strong isolationist sentiment in the Congress, promised support and supplies but no troops. Soon, however, every young American male was talking about joining one of the military services. They wanted to serve their country in case we did get into the war.

As 1941 approached, I was in the senior class in the Fort Deposit high school, and was going to graduate in May. I was a tall, physically strong young man, a forward on the basketball team and a tackle in football. I was ready to take on any challenge, or so I believed. All I could think about was how I wanted to go, see, and do all the things I had never seen or done before. I was developing a real wanderlust.

I worked several afternoon and weekend jobs. For a while I was the Greyhound bus agent in our town and pumped gas for a penny a gallon. I had built up a good business and was making more money than the average man with a family to support. With this money, I bought a 1938 Harley-Davidson motorcycle that gave me the ability to go anywhere I wanted. I traveled to small towns within fifty miles of home and would take the girls for a ride, making some quick stops, telling them to hold on tight. If they didn't, I would not take them again.

I was a daredevil and would ride as fast as 60 miles an hour standing up in the seat. Once, at the state fair, I took my Harley on a dare inside the cylinder where cyclists would ride round and round up the inside wall until they reached the top lip of the cylinder, depending on centrifugal force to keep the wheels of their bikes pressed firmly to the sides to prevent them from falling to the bottom. Somehow I managed—I'll never know quite how—to do this trick riding without killing myself.

THERE ARE CERTAIN EVENTS that, against all expectation, change one's life. So it was with me. It was near the end of the school year, and the senior prom was coming. I asked my best and only female friend, whom we will call Jamie, to go with me. Jamie was brunette, beautiful, and sixteen years old. She and I had shared almost everything since we were in the first grade together. Jamie was dating a boy from another city and was glad we could go together, because her beau could not come to the prom. I didn't know how close they were, but I was glad she would let me take her. I asked my dad if I could use his car because it wouldn't be possible to take her on the bike in her formal dress.

When the time came to leave for the prom, I asked for the car keys. Dad gave them to me, telling me I would have to buy some gas. I looked to see how much gas there was, and the gauge was on empty. When I told Dad about this, he said, "Well, you will have to furnish your own gas. You have enough money to keep that bike on the road all the time."

I didn't have enough money to buy gas and to take my date out with the others after the prom was over. It was too embarrassing to go to her house this late and tell her I could not be her prom date that night, so I did not go at all. I felt like a heel. I just got on my bike and rode up and down the road thinking about how to face Jamie and my classmates again.

Somehow, Jamie forgave me. She told me, though, that she was going to her boyfriend's home on the Fourth of July holiday to meet his parents. Man, that blew my mind. I thought she was going to become engaged to marry him. The night before she was to go, I asked her to go to a movie with me. When I questioned her, she told me that her boyfriend was getting serious about her. Thoughts raced through my mind about the fact that Jamie was about to leave me and get married.

I was in no mood for a movie, so we didn't go. We rode my bike to a lover's lane where we had gone many times. When I kissed her, it was like bells and whistles going off, because I had never kissed her on the lips before. The same feeling came over her. We locked arm in arm kissing and crying like two little kids.

For the first time in our lives we knew that our relationship was more than just a friendship. We were deeply in love and could not turn each other loose. This went on for four hours or so. The tears flowed down our faces and we spoke words of love and promised each other that we would not part. She told me that her trip would only be a friendship trip and that she would tell this boy that she could not marry him. That was not good enough for me. I told her that if she went on the trip, I would not be there when she returned.

As the time passed for us to go home, we sat there holding and kissing each other. It was 3 a.m. before we looked at our watches. When we drove to her house, the lights were on and her mother was waiting on the porch. As her mother looked at us, Jamie said to me,

"I'm not going."

When we got up on the porch her mother asked, "Where on earth have you been?" She turned to her mother and said, "I'm not going."

Her mother said, "Oh, yes, you are. You do not make promises to someone and break the promise without good cause." Then her mother turned to me and said, "I think you had better go right now. She is going on this trip, I don't care what she has said."

The night was a sleepless one for me. I was afraid that if I went to bed I would miss going to the train station at 7 a.m. to see if she really was going to leave. Sure enough, at 7 a.m. her mother drove up to the station. My heart dropped when I saw my Jamie board the train. I felt as though my heart would explode, and I could not hold back the tears. As the train clanked to a start and the engineer blew the whistle, it was like my world had come to an end. I knew then just how much I loved her.

By the time I got on my bike the tears had turned to anger. I told myself that I would not be there when she returned and rode as fast as I could back home. After changing clothes I hung my hat on the hall hat rack and took only a change of underclothes with me because I was not sure where I was going. I remember someone said something to me, but I didn't stop to answer. I just jumped on my bike and stormed off down the road. The farther I rode, the angrier I got. Before I knew what I wanted to do or where I wanted to go, I was in Montgomery.

The gas tank was full, so riding around kept my mind occupied for a while. I wondered if any of my friends were at the naval recruiting office. All the boys that could get their folks to sign for them were going into the service instead of looking for a job. I decided to check it out.

When I arrived at the recruiting office no boys from my hometown were there, so I went to a juke joint where we always went when we came to Montgomery. The owner of the club had told us not to come in there by ourselves because the local boys would pick a fight with us. We had to go in groups of four or more and that was usually after dark. I thought it would be all right to go during the day, so I went on in and found a few guys and gals there.

I walked over by the dance floor and ordered a Coke. As I sat there wondering what to do about the situation between Jamie and me, the owner walked over and said in a rough, loud voice, "I told you Lowndes County boys not to come in here by yourselves. The guys over there are talking about beating you up. Get the heck out of here!"

I told him I would leave as soon as I drank my Coke. He grabbed the Coke and said, "Get out now, and do not come back by yourself again."

As I walked to my bike the anger was building up inside. I got on my bike and started toward the road. All of a sudden the resentment was more than I could bear. I turned the bike around and headed for the club's swinging doors. By the time I reached the doors, I was going about 45 mph on that bike.

The crash bars on the bike took out the right door, sending it into the table and chairs like a missile. As I headed for the big dance floor in the back, the bike made a path through the table and chairs, sending pieces flying across the room.

The guys and girls in the juke joint were running and screaming. When I reached the dance floor, I speeded up, did a figure eight, then I stopped in the middle of the dance floor, shot the gas to it so that the back wheel would make a streak all the way across the dance floor. I headed toward the door through another row of table and chairs, demolishing them.

As I looked toward the bar I saw the owner coming out of his office with a shotgun. Before he could round the corner I was through the left door, taking it out and sending it into the parking lot. I realized that if I went to the road I might have to stop for cars, so I turned and went around the building, through bushes and tall grass across a ditch, up a bank, and into the street. I was out of sight before he could draw a bead on me.

Down the street I stopped at a gas station. I knew the owner and told him what I had done.

He said, "Boy, you are in serious trouble. That man is mean. He will hunt you down and shoot you like a dog."

As I rode away I was wondering how I would ever get out of this mess. My first idea was to get out of town. My girlfriend was on her way to get married, and I had done an awful thing in that nightclub. My thoughts were so confused that I didn't realize where I was until I noticed that the Army-Navy Recruiting Offices were in the shopping strip I was passing. "Well," I said to myself, "I think it's time to try the army."

Since I looked older than I was and in order not to have my parents sign for me, I would tell the recruiter I was twenty-one. Now, to make it look good, I had to pick a date of birth. So I picked the 3rd of July to be my new birth date.

I walked into the recruiting office and a sergeant came over to greet me. When he asked what I wanted, I told him that I wanted to join up. He asked how old I was and this is when the words just came out: "It's my birthday, I'm 21 today." Within an hour all the paperwork was done and a lieutenant came out of his office and swore me in. He said, "You are in the Army now. Happy birthday."

They gave me three options as to where I wanted to go. I chose the Philippine Islands because Alaska was too cold and the Panama Canal was too close to Montgomery. I knew it would take the bar owner time to find me with that shotgun if I went all the way to the Philippine Islands.

By now my anger was replaced with the thought that my girlfriend would be surprised when she returned to find that I'd gone away. I did not expect her to come back engaged to her boyfriend, and I also thought she might wait for me, but a three-year enlistment is a long time. Anyway, it was too late to change things now.

The recruiter gave me a train ticket to Hattiesburg, Mississippi, with orders to go to Camp Shelby, one meal ticket, and a phone number to call when I arrived to let camp officials know to pick me up. I went to my cousin's house to give him my bike. To keep him from knowing where I was going, I got him to drop me off at the bus station. My thought was that if he knew I was going by train, he would suspect I was going on a longer trip, and I did not want to make him suspicious. I told him he could ride my bike because I might not be back for a month or so.

I WAS WAITING FOR the train to Hattiesburg when the lieutenant from the recruiting office came into the station and gave me a brown envelope with orders for two black recruits to report to Camp Shelby. He told me these were my first orders and to see that these two guys got off in Hattiesburg and went with me when I got picked up by the men from Camp Shelby.

At the very first stop, the two guys were trying to get off the train, so I had to walk back to their car to make sure they stayed on. Every stop we made they tried to get off until we arrived in Hattiesburg the next morning. When I got back to their car, both were sound asleep. When we got off and I made the phone call to Camp Shelby, the officials told me I was not to arrive until the 5th, informing me that this was the Fourth of July. After making that five-cent phone call, all I had left was twenty cents, and I only had one meal ticket.

The two black men asked me to get them something to eat. When I talked to the station restaurant manager he agreed to feed the two black men, but told me that I should have had better sense than to leave Montgomery without any money. He fed them, but not me. There I was, spending the Fourth of July broke when back home we always had a big dinner and plenty of watermelon to celebrate the holiday.

The camp officials did not show up until late in the afternoon. When I told them that we hadn't had anything to eat since I had been given only one meal ticket they informed me that the mess hall was closed, but when we got to the camp, they made us some sandwiches.

I turned in the papers on the two men, and then I was taken to a tent where I was to remain until they processed us out. The tent was one of those semi-permanent ones with a canvas top and a wooden floor, with three feet of wood siding and wire screening up to the roof. It was large enough for eight bunk beds. The edge of the canvas had several ropes that anchored into the ground. When it rained we would have to tighten the ropes to keep the rain from collapsing the tent.

I met my first hard-nosed drill sergeant at Camp Shelby. His name was Jones, but we called him Bulldog. At 6 a.m. every day he would blow that whistle loud enough to hear five blocks away. He would also yell, "All right, you dogfaces. Up and at 'em." When he blew that whistle the spit would fly about three yards from his mouth. I never saw anyone else that could blow a whistle and yell at the same time. He would also walk alongside the tents, beating on them with a stick.

He stayed on us all the time. His yelling and blowing that whistle was as bad as the stink on a wet dog. You could not do anything to please him. I asked him why he yelled so much, his answer was, "This is the army, and you isn't seen nothing yet. You dogfaces will have to shape up or ship out."

To get up and outside in fifteen minutes was hard to do, but you dared not come out with your shirttail hanging out or your shoes untied. He gave us new guys instructions and said anyone who didn't follow them would be placed on KP, which, I was told later, meant Kitchen Police. It didn't sound so bad to me, but later I found out it was hard work cleaning up the mess hall, peeling potatoes, or doing anything else the mess sergeant needed.

In July in that part of Mississippi it rained almost every afternoon, maybe even three or four times. The minute the rain started, the sergeant would blow that whistle and yell, "All out to tighten the ropes on the tent." Then the rain would stop and here he would come yelling for us to loosen the tent ropes. That could happen several times a day, and usually did.

When we were not on KP, the sergeant would take us on other work details, which was fine for me. I didn't want to sit around and listen to a bunch of draftees complain all the time. I guess I heard about every story in the book from them.

When we went to get our first uniforms, we had to pass by a big long counter with about four men grabbing shirts, pants, GI underwear, shoes, and socks out of boxes. No thought was given to size; you got whatever was next. Bulldog, the drill sergeant, said, "Stop bitching. Trade with each other to get a better fit or wear what you were given."

I've never seen such a motley-looking bunch as we were when we turned out that evening to march to mess hall. Some had shirts that looked like gunnysacks with pants that were too long and had to be rolled up. Some pants were too short and hitched about a foot up their legs. I couldn't get a cap to fit me, so they gave me a cavalry hat that was World War I issue. The worst thing was trying to look like regular soldiers for inspection the next day. When the captain came to inspect the troops he was flabbergasted. "Sergeant, where did these men get their clothing?"

His answer was, "GI issue, sir."

The captain said, "Please hide them until I can get something done."

It took about four days before we got to trade in shirts, shoes, and pants for a better fit, but we still looked like rejects from a used clothing store. We stayed that way until our orders came to ship out. Then we got better-fitting clothes for the trip to California.

What a wonderful thing to get orders to get out of Camp Shelby. There were twenty-five of us going to Angel Island, California, in the San Francisco Bay area. We were loaded onto Pullman cars with a buck sergeant in charge. They gave us a ten dollar advance pay so we would have a little pocket change.

We were glad to be on our way. Some of the men were going to Hawaii, some to Guam, and a few, like me, to the Philippines. All of us Alabama, North Florida, and Mississippi boys were thrilled with the idea of travelling west. Our route would take us through Louisiana, Texas, New Mexico, Colorado, Utah, and Nevada into California—places we had never seen before. It was exciting to cross the great Mississippi River at Baton Rouge, Louisiana, then travel on to the big city of Dallas, Texas.

At times my thoughts would drift back to home, wondering if Jamie had returned without being engaged to marry. Thoughts of my family not knowing where I was would surface, for I had been very careful not to tell anyone that I had joined the Army, using a false birth date for fear they would find out I was only sixteen and send me back home.

As we traveled west into the Texas Panhandle, the land was bare. I never thought one could look so far without seeing trees. One night somewhere in northern New Mexico we were told that our Pullman cars would be side railed to wait for another train to pick us up. When we woke up the next morning I looked out the window and could not see a single tree, all the way to the horizon. There were mountains in the background. It was like we had landed on the moon. I woke everyone saying, "Look fellows, there are no trees in sight." All of them peeped out the window. In a few minutes everyone was outside looking in every direction with all kinds of comments.

About an hour later a train came and hooked up our cars. We were going through Colorado, and soon we were amazed at the sight of the Rocky Mountains. Our seven-day trip from Camp Shelby to California was one of amazing beauty for us Southern boys.

When we arrived at the train station in San Francisco, our sergeant told us to stay in the terminal and not go anywhere, not even outside the building. After about an hour, four of us walked outside just to see what we could of San Francisco. As we stood there four men came around the corner of the building. They were walking straight toward us dressed in red, white and blue uniforms with all kinds of brass buttons. We had never seen anyone so dressed up. As they approached, being southern born and raised, we spoke to them, "Hello, how are you all?"

They did not speak a word. The next thing we knew we were knocked down against the wall, and each one of us had a busted nose or our eyes were swelling shut. Our ribs were hurting. They still didn't say a word, just laughed and walked down the sidewalk. As we were getting up trying to get back into the railroad terminal, the sergeant came up and asked what happened. We told our story, and he smiled, and said, "You have just met the U.S. Marine Corps." They knew we were recruits by the sloppy way we were dressed.

The sergeant had arranged our transportation by ferry to Angel Island. When we arrived it was dark, but it was a much better place than Camp Shelby. Hundreds of men were there waiting for ships to the Far East. Most were recruits, like us, headed to the Far East for a hitch of three years.

It didn't take long before I met some interesting guys. Most of the men in our barracks were going to Hawaii to Hickam Field and were in the Army Air Corps. There were men from all parts of the U.S.A., and most were volunteer regular Army like me. There were no draftees there that I could find.

When I found the bunk that I had been assigned, the guy bunking next to me was a person I will never forget. I'll call him Hal. Hal had joined the Army instead of letting them draft him and was going to the Philippine Islands, the same as I was. He bitched about everything. When I told him I did not smoke, he had a fit that they had assigned someone next to him who had no money, didn't smoke, and that he could not bum smokes from.

Hal was the best panhandler I had ever run into. He would walk up to anyone and ask for a cigarette, promising to pay the person back when he got a payday. He would do what we call "shoot butts on the ground," gathering enough to roll a smoke. He would complain about not having proper paper to roll his smokes. He calculated that on army pay it would take him six months to pay back everyone that he had bummed a smoke from.

The officers lined us up for inspection and looked us over, then most of us were told to go get a haircut. Haircuts were twenty-five cents at the camp barbershop. Most of the guys didn't have any money, so the officers put in for us to get a partial pay of ten dollars. Man, that ten bucks looked like a million dollars.

Hal went to the PX and got a carton of smokes, stuck them in his army bag, and put just a couple of cigarettes in his shirt pocket. When he met this guy he had bummed a smoke from, the guy asked him for a smoke back. Hal told him he didn't have one yet. Then Hal turned to me and said, "See, that's why I won't carry a pack with me. All these bums would want their smokes paid back!"

One day he walked up to a guy and bummed a smoke, and I asked him why. I knew he had some in his pocket. He said it was because he didn't want to forget how to do it, since another partial pay might not come until we were in the Philippine Islands.

We were required to get that haircut. By the time we got to the barbershop, there was a line about two blocks long. Hal bitched all the way until he got into the chair. He told the barber that he had waited in a line a mile long, and it sure was nice to get to sit down. Hal started to tell him how he wanted his hair cut. By the time he got the words out of his mouth, the barber took the barber sheet from around his neck and yelled, "Next!"

Hal looked in the mirror and saw his bald head. He told the barber he hadn't cut it like he wanted it, and he said he wanted his quarter back.

"You want to get out or you want me to put you out?" the barber said. So Hal slowly walked out the door complaining about what a rip-off that haircut had been.

As we walked back to our bunks we met a captain and a lieutenant. Hal put up both hands and gave them a double salute. The captain asked him, "Why did you use both hands?"

Hal said, "Well, there were two of you."

They made him stand there and using one hand, go through the exercise about ten times. When we walked off Hal said he knew how to salute correctly, but did it the other way for the hell of it. There were no dull days with Hal around. He was always doing something to buck the system.

When the officials came around asking if anyone wanted to set up an allotment to himself in the Bank of America so when you arrived back in America you would have some money, Hal said that eleven dollars a month would not keep him in smokes, so he declined. I figured that a three-year hitch at ten dollars per month would help when I arrived back in the States. We had already been told that things were cheap in the Philippine Islands.

ANGEL ISLAND WAS BETTER than Camp Shelby, but it was hard getting adjusted to Army life. I watched the bulletin board each day to see if I had shipping orders. After eleven days my name came up. I was assigned to the USS Cleveland, a converted passenger liner being used as a troop ship. Some of the troops were going to Hawaii, some to Guam, and the rest of us to the Philippine Islands.

It was a wonderful sight to sail under the Golden Gate Bridge that afternoon. As we looked back at the mountains fading out of sight, I choked up inside. Standing on the fantail, I thought of home, my girlfriend, and the club owner, wondering if he had tried to find me. I was also thinking about my mother. No one knew where I was. I was going to a different world, to a strange land, to live among people I knew nothing about. For better or for worse, I was leaving my native country behind, ready, I thought, for whatever lay ahead.

— 2 —

Last Days of Innocence

CROSSING THE PACIFIC OCEAN aboard the President Cleveland proved to be quite an adventure. Some mornings the water would be as slick as glass with not a wave to be seen. Before we got to Guam, though, we went through a storm where the waves came over the side of the ship, with some of them breaking all the way over us. Almost everyone on board got sick. I spent many hours just thinking about what had happened before I left the States. Sometimes I wished that I were back home. I was feeling homesick as well as seasick.

As we approached the Philippines and sailed through the Manila Straits we could see dense jungle off both sides of the ship. Looking out over Manila itself, we could make out a green countryside with a high-rise building towering above the trees. Soon we could see the outline of the Pasic River that ran through the city. I was looking forward to exploring this new country and getting to know its people and their ways. Meeting people was always something I liked.

We docked at the pier in Manila on a very hot day with the sun blasting down on us from a cloudless, hazy sky. A band was playing, and some Filipinos were dancing in the streets to greet the Americans. We could hardly wait to join them, since we had been at sea for what seemed a very long time. When we disembarked we were told that an army or air corps unit would come to pick us up. At that point there were seven of us going to Nichols Field to the air wing. I told Hal goodbye, and we made plans to see each other later.

It took us about an hour to get off the ship and into the parking lot. Trucks came and picked up everyone else, but no one came for those of us assigned to Nichols Field. All around us were army guys yelling "31st Infantry" and the names and numbers of different units, but no one yelled out the name of ours. Soon the lot was empty, and there we stood, seven men in the middle of an empty parking lot, not knowing where to go. We felt abandoned and somewhat lost, but displayed the usual male bravado as we joked and waited. And waited.

Finally a jeep came by, and we were asked where we were supposed to go. Then we waited for another hour before trucks arrived to pick us up. We found out that the air wing to which we had been assigned was out on maneuvers. We were to be taken to the 75th Ordinance Company for housing until our wing came back.

To our surprise the ordinance location was just a mile from the docks. The 75th Ordinance Company was an old army unit set up along with others after the Spanish lost control of the Philippine Islands at the turn of the century. The company's job was to supply ammunition and services to the Philippine Department of the Army, and included a machine shop to rebuild ordinance equipment. The machine shop itself was located in Fort Santiago, within the Walled City of old Manila.

The barracks were apparently the same as the Spanish Army had used and included a mess hall, barber shop, orderly room, and a PX, with the sleeping quarters upstairs. The PX was owned by the 75th Ordinance and its profits went for programs, parties, or functions for the 135 men in the company. The men of the 75th consisted mostly of soldiers who had ten or more years in the service, and it was almost impossible for anyone else to get into the unit. Many of them were married to Filipino women and had children. They would retire and stay in the islands the rest of their lives. Many had never been back to America since they arrived for their first hitch.

The 75th's commander was Colonel George Hurst. He was a wonderful soldier, and First Sgt. Warren was an easygoing type person who could get along with anybody. The men of the 75th worked a half-day while in Manila and could go anywhere they wanted. But on field trips to Bataan they worked from sun-up to sundown. By the time I got there, the Dept. of Engineers was building warehouses on Bataan and the 75th was filling them with ordinance. It was common knowledge that if war came, that's where we would go.

When we arrived at the company barracks, our welcoming party consisted of Master Sergeant Warren and two drunks. We were given a few rules, but our general impression was that this location was going to be a wonderful place to be—and right downtown. We were not expected to do any work, since the company had Filipinos as KP. Imagine that, no KP! We were required to fall out with the company every day, but right after morning roll call, we were dismissed.

Our first pass came that weekend. We had heard many stories about Manila—its Benny Boys, girls, and cab drivers. We were also told not to go alone when visiting the town because the natives all knew when new recruits arrived and would be sure to try to take advantage of us. I looked our group over to pick out some suitably husky companions for a venture into town. My choices were the farm boy from Minnesota and another guy from South Dakota. We figured three of us were enough to keep each other safe. We had almost no money, but that didn't matter. Things were very cheap.

As we began walking towards town, four cabs were following us, and we hopped in the first one behind us. It was like stepping into a rocket. No sooner had the doors slammed shut than the driver took off on the wrong side of the street towards the bridge leading into the town, the horn blaring every inch of the way. He missed a light pole by about a quarter of an inch. It seemed as though every cab in town was trying to get over that bridge side by side.

Somehow we managed to make it to the Manila side without losing an arm or a leg. It was the wildest ride I had ever had, and I wished I were back in Alabama sitting on my old mule and enjoying his smooth, unhurried gait. As we got out of the cab, my two friends fervently thanked God the ride was over, and that we had survived it. We all agreed that walking back to the barracks was our best bet.

Exploring the streets of Manila, we were surrounded by the exotic smells of the unfamiliar foods being cooked. Peddlers crowded around us trying to sell us whatever they had. Little kids were pimping for their "mothers" or "sisters," and would beg us to go to their house for ten pesos, or would reduce the price to five pesos if we didn't take their first offer. There were two famous massage parlors that most servicemen went into because they could get about anything they wanted there. From the grunts, groans, and laughs we could hear behind the thin walls, I could believe it. We skipped that entertainment.

We decided to go to a place we had heard of called the Poodle Dog Club. As we went through the door, it looked like everyone else was leaving, and leaving in a hurry. Chairs were flying through the air and tables were falling in pieces to the floor. A big fight was in progress, with soldiers and sailors at it hard and heavy. Whistles were blowing, and soon the MPs and SPs were all over the place. Nearly everyone scrammed out one of the three doors leading to the streets. The MPs and SPs didn't take anyone in. They just told the bartender they would stay close in case the guys came back. We found out that about every thirty minutes a good fight would break out—just part of the atmosphere of the Poodle Dog Club.

We ambled on to the Southeastern Hotel and decided to visit a bar on the top floor that was famous for a drink called the Gally-wacker, made with several shots of whisky, rum, rice wine, and God knows what else. As we walked in we noticed yellow lines about two feet apart leading from the bar to the cashier. If you could drink two Gallywackers, it was said, and walk to the cashier without stepping on the yellow lines, the two drinks were free.

One of us was a guy from Texas who said he wanted to try to drink the Gallywackers and make it all the way to the cashier. All the rest of us drank San Miguel beer. After Tex drank his second Gallywacker he sat there bragging about how he wasn't drunk and how he could walk the yellow lines without a bobble. As he got up from his chair, his legs would not hold him up. He fell flat on the floor, and had to have a couple of us help him to his feet. We held him up and guided him to the lines. When we turned him loose, he went backwards into the bar. The bartender came over and explained to Tex that you had to go forward, not backwards, to win the two drinks. It took us about twenty minutes to get him out of the bar, down the elevator, and into the street.

When, after another wild taxi ride, we arrived at the front door of our compound Tex was sober up top, but his legs still would not function very well. We took him up to his bunk on the second floor and he slept until the next day.

My PAY WAS TWENTY-ONE dollars a month, less the ten dollars I put in the Bank of America. This left me only eleven dollars a month of spending money, but since the rate of exchange was two pesos to the dollar, I had twenty-two pesos a month to spend. Beer was ten centa-vos—or five cents American money—at our PX, so soon we were drink-ing San Miguel beer for our main alcoholic beverage. For six pesos a month, the company had hired a group of Filipinos to do all KP, clothes washing, hair cutting, shoe shining, and cleaning up the barracks. It was like a luxury hotel.

On our seventh day of waiting for our air wing to get back, Sgt. Warren called us all down to the day room. He said he had room for us to transfer to the 75th if we wanted to. Most of us had not taken our boot camp training. We had seen the poor suckers who came over with us on the USS Cleveland marching up and down the 31st Infantry parade field sweating and swearing. We had no desire to undergo that kind of training when our air wing came back, so Sgt. Warren didn't have to twist our arms to get us to sign up.

He also told us we could go to the Ordinance Training School instead of boot camp, and the ones with grades of 80 or above could become Ordinance Officers in the Philippine Dept. and be assigned to a Philippine Island Army base. If we served three years, we would be eligible to go to Officers' Candidate School when we returned to the U.S. This sounded like a good deal. An officer made a lot more money than an enlisted man. We all thought we should consider this option.

GERALD, LUKE, AND I made friends with one of the Filipino bosses at the depot, a guy named Vargas. He liked us and invited us to go with him on weekend trips. He had been a guide in the Philippine Islands at one time and knew where to fish, hunt, and all about everything else there was to do for recreation.

On our next weekend off we decided to take one of the personnel carriers and go on a wild boar hunt. The PX fund would furnish the gas. That was one of the things we were allowed to do with the profits from the PX. We were armed with old 1906 .45 caliber revolvers that were used against the Hucks before World War II. We also got permission to check out M-I carbines for our hunting trip.

Vargas took us into heavy jungle in the Bataan area with extreme-ly narrow roads. We were stopped a few times by Filipino men asking us where we were going. Vargas would talk to them in their language, and they would tell him the best places to hunt wild boar. As we went deeper into the jungle, the guide spotted a sow with piglets off to our left. We did not know it, but the boar of this little family was just across the trail from the sow and her piglets and that he was nothing if not mean. We had all gotten out of our vehicle when we heard that wild boar charging us from behind.

An angry wild boar is not to be trifled with. We all started yell-ing and running around the personnel carrier shooting our 45s at the boar, which was attacking the tires on the truck and chasing all of us. We scrambled back into the relative safety that the truck offered, climbing over each other to do it. Most of us had fired our 45s at least once or twice. Vargas was yelling at us. There was no way, he said, that he was going to stay in the woods with us shooting like wild men, so we decided to end the wild boar hunt and drive north to visit some villages, and maybe go into the hills and visit a Negrito tribe.

We drove into a small village where kids ran out into the street to see us, waving at us. When the truck stopped, Vargas told us the kids had never seen American soldiers before. All the people in the village came out to look. The older folks talked to us and to our guide, and some of the kids came up and touched our skin. It was as though we were movie stars, and we got a big kick out of it.

As we drove out of town all the kids ran along behind us waving and yelling. The folks in town had told us how to get to the Negrito village up in the mountains. As we negotiated the winding road, mon-keys were high in the trees, screaming at us. They were telling other monkeys further up that danger was coming their way. It was so funny to us. It was the first time I had seen monkeys in the wild. It looked as if there were hundreds of them. When we had driven as far up the trail as possible, we got out and walked the rest of the way to the village. He said that the Negritos already knew someone was coming because of the noise the monkeys were making.

Vargas met two men who were about four feet high and had gray hair, one of them being the head of the tribe. He talked to Vargas for a few minutes, then he told us we were welcome to their village. The natives both carried a bolo, a long knife like a machete. As we walked into the village we saw there were eight grass shacks with a clearing in the center. Five or six kids came out from each shack. Several women and some younger men stared curiously at us.

They would not come close to us at first. When the old men told them to come out and greet us they came forward and made a motion that seemed to be a sign of welcome. They told Vargas they thought we were giants. We found out that only one of them had ever been down the hill to the village, and none had ever been to a town of any size.

THE NEXT WEEKEND VARGAS invited me to go with him to a province south of Manila to meet some of his friends and family. We rode the train about twenty-five miles to a small town where we were met at the station by his brother and several of his friends. On our way to the brother's house, Vargas told me he wanted me to meet a nice Filipino girl who was not like the ones in Manila.

Soon there were about five girls close to my age at the house. As I was introduced to them, my friend got to this one girl and turned to me saying, "This is a very special girl I want you to meet. Her name is Nelda." Nelda was pretty and very nicely dressed. Her hair was long, and she had a beautiful smile. As she spoke to me she said, "I've heard a lot of good things about you," in perfect English.

I thanked her, and she invited me to the dining table for some lemonade.

The table was covered with fruit and other things grown there. The main dish was to be a barbecued pig that they were already cooking out in the backyard. The barbecuing technique was rather special. They would put the pig in a small pen that restricted its movement and feed it all it could eat until it was as fat as they wanted it. Then they gave it a laxative to clean it out. When the pig was cleaned out they would feed the pig rice with highly seasoned sauce to flavor the meat. The minute the pig stuffed himself with the rice, they would kill it. Then they would run a steel rod down its mouth and all the way through the pig, hang the rod and pig above a fire, and roast the whole thing. And I must say the meat was wonderful.

After we ate, Nelda and I went to a park a few blocks away. I could tell she liked me more than any of the girls I had met in Manila. When we left the park she wanted me to go to her house and meet her family. With that thought in mind I drifted to memories of back home. Could I be doing the same as my girl Jamie, meeting the family, but not making any commitment?

As we walked into the house she introduced me to her father. Nelda said, "Dad, this is my new friend, a U.S. Army private from the 75th Ordinance that was brought here by our friend. This is the soldier he talked to you about."

Her father thanked me for coming and asked that I have a seat. Then her mother came into the room, and she also gave me a great welcome. Then came her three brothers and two sisters. They were all fine-looking people. All were well mannered and welcomed me. They asked where I was from in America and about my family, and we talked for a while.

As we walked back to the other house, Nelda asked if we could stop at the park again. She said she wanted to show me something.

At the far end of the park was a large wire cage, inside of which were several monkeys. As we stood looking at the monkeys, she pointed out the mother monkey and the father and said they were married and all the others were their children. She looked up at me and asked if I wanted to get married some day. My answer was, "Sure." She said she liked Americans and could be very happy if she were married to one.

I knew Nelda liked me, but I could not stop thinking about Jamie. I told myself that I could not let myself get involved with anyone until I knew what my Jamie had done. But I pulled Nelda close to me for a small kiss. As we kissed she held me tight and said that mine was the sweetest kiss she had ever had. I knew right then we had better get back to her house. Our original plans were to stay down there Saturday night, but when we reached the house, Vargas said we had to go back to our base. At that point it was fine with me.

The following Wednesday afternoon Sgt. Warren called me to the day room. When I got there Nelda was there. She said she had come to Manila, and she wanted to see me. As pretty as she was I was proud to take her to the PX and show her off to the guys in the company. She got along well with other people and was not a standoffish kind of person. I liked that about her.

A WORK DETAIL TO Bataan was on the schedule. We were not sure that any of us new guys would get to go but the older guys told us they wanted us to go and that they would work the hell out of us. That Saturday came with an order on the day room board listing everyone who would go early on Monday. All seven of us were on it. Our friend, Tex, didn't want to go. He said he would go and get drunk so he could stay in Manila, and at the time of the Monday morning 6 a.m. wake-up call, Tex was so drunk he had to be carried to the truck. Sgt. Warren told us to load him into the back of one of the trucks and throw his footlocker in with him.

It was a long haul—130 miles—to our Bataan post from Manila. I was one of the drivers and found it hard going. The roads were part gravel and very rough and dusty. We drove big Corbit trucks with tandem back wheels, the biggest trucks I had ever driven. We camped out under large jungle trees in pup tents, two persons to a tent. Not quite the same type of accommodation that we were used to in Manila. Our supply warehouses were close by. Our mess hall, as we called it, was a wooden floored tent with a canvas top and no doors or windows.

Our job was to unload barges of ammo into our truck and take them to the seventy warehouses in the jungle that the engineers had built for us and seventy more for the quartermasters. As we were unloading, I asked the sergeant-in-charge why the quartermaster corps wasn't putting supplies into its own warehouses. He told me that the colonel had ordered that the ammo go directly into our field warehouses so we would not have to re-handle it.

My thoughts would often drift back to home and my folks. They had no idea that I was in the Philippine Islands 10,000 miles away from Lowndes County. No one at home knew for sure where I was, so I did write and mail a letter when I got back to Manila.

The rains came, and we kept working, loading bombs—500 pound ones. Sometimes we had to pull a truck uphill with a bulldozer, but nothing stopped us. We had a great many tons to load, and the quicker we got it done the quicker we could go back to the easy life in Manila.

As it got close to December, our trips to downtown Manila began to include bars. The Marouka Bar was where Japanese came to drink, and most of the time a few Japanese sailors would be in there. The jukebox had keys and when you pushed down a key you could flip back up and change it before the record would play. We would put our dime in to play a song. As soon as we went to our table, the Japs would come up and change it to some Japanese record they preferred. One night there were about twenty to thirty Japanese sailors in the club. We went back to our company and told the others about the many Japs that were there and what they were doing. We scraped up all the money we could so everyone could have enough for a couple of beers. We went into the club in groups of four or five. When our company was all inside, we went to the jukebox and played a few re-cords, then the Japs came and pushed up our keys and played a Jap song. The minute the song started we all got up and grabbed the near-est Jap to us. Sometimes there were two on one. We broke up all the tables, chairs, mirrors, and the bar. We beat the bartender and laid out all the Japs on the floor. If one started to get up he would be hit in the head with a beer bottle.

When we heard the police, the MPs and the SPs coming in the front and starting up the stairs, we all went out the back down onto the roof, then to the street, and faded away into the dark. No one was caught. When we were notified that the MPs would be around with the bartender to identify the ones that beat him, the guilty parties were sent to Bataan real quick. The last we heard about the situation was that the Japs wanted the army to pay for the damage to the bar.

It had been some time before we arrived that the company had had their last beer party at the compound. Now, Sergeant Warren talked the commanding officer into having another one for us before we had to go back to Bataan. KP boys were to serve beer and handle a big dinner for us. We could invite one person to the party if we wished.

As we were eating, a guy that I had had some words with was sitting across the table from me. He started putting olives on a knife and flipping them across the table at me. I told him to stop. He kept on, so I reached over the table and dragged him over onto my side, and we started to fight.

Everyone was half drunk. A group got around me to hold me, and some also got around him. He soon got loose from them, picked up a butcher knife and, running at me, stuck it in my groin about four inches deep. The knife had cut a main artery, and blood was spouting all over the place. They got a truck and put me in the back and one guy held the artery closed all the way to Ft. William McKinley Hospital. Had he not known to do this I would have been history.

I sent word to Vargas about the knifing, and he told Nelda. The next day she came to the hospital to see me. She was crying as though I wouldn't make it. I asked that she be permitted to stay and take care of me. When they wouldn't let her stay, she got real upset, but within a week I was out and back at the company compound.

I HAD ENROLLED IN the ordinance school and program, and between going to school and the work on Bataan I stayed busy. To get away in the afternoon I would go down the street and sit and watch all the boats go up and down the Pasic River. I would sit and think about all the things that were happening to me and wonder why I had not heard from home. It was getting close to December 1st, my seventeenth birthday, and still I heard nothing. I guess I could understand my family not communicating with me since I had run away in the first place.

As luck would have it, our Bataan detail was to pull out the last day of November, 1941. That meant I would be in Bataan on my birthday and miss the party Nelda had planned for me. When I told her we were leaving, she cried and cried.

Though no one knew precisely where it came from, a cloud of uncertainty—or maybe apprehension—seemed to be hovering around us. We could not quite define it, but it was hard to say goodbye that morning as we pulled out of Manila. It was a pretty day, and, looking at the road lined by the waving natives, I thought how good they were for our morale, smiling and waving at us. I would toot the horn, and everyone, including the older folks, would wave at me. They were such happy-go-lucky people you couldn't help but like them. If you stopped to talk, they would take you home with them for dinner,

When we arrived in Bataan we were told that it would take us at least two weeks to handle all the ammo that had come in: 500 lb. bombs, 30 lb. fragment bombs, and 100 lb. bombs, something we hadn't had in Bataan before. Most of our ammo was shells, 155 and 75 mm, so we were surprised at what was being sent to us.

It was, as usual, hard work from sunrise to sundown every day. At night in camp we would play cards or sit around and tell stories, jokes, or talk about our families and friends back home. Everyone would kid me about being from Alabama. I would always come back saying that it was the number one state. That would get a big Rah-Rah. Well, I said, look at the list of the states, and Alabama is always the first one. So it had to be number one.

As we sat in that jungle camp kidding each other and swapping stories deep into the night, we had no way to know that the next day our lives would be changed forever.

— 3 —

The War Comes

THE MORNING SEEMED LIKE any other morning: time to get up, get dressed, and go to work. It was December 8th in the Philippines. In Hawaii it was Sunday, December 7th, 1941.

I was getting my big truck ready to roll out when I heard a lot of yelling in the midst of great commotion. Sergeant Debouch was shouting for everyone to come to the orderly room, and Sergeant Mahoney was beating the chow bell. We knew there must be something big happening and took off running to see what it was.

After we were all inside and the noise had died down a little, we were told that the Japanese had bombed Pearl Harbor and were expected to attack the Philippine Islands at any time. We were told to go to the docks and get all the ammunition that was there, transport it to our warehouses and check regularly for any change in orders.

As I sat on the dock waiting to have ammo loaded into my truck, I tried to understand what was happening. Were we all going to be involved in a full-blown war with Japan? I didn't think it was really possible. As my mind raced from one thought to another my entire past and present went through my mind. Of all the places in the world I could be, I figured, right here in the Philippines was the worst. Why had I chosen to come here? I thought about the Marouka bar fight with the Japanese sailors and wished we had killed all of them. How could those Japs dare start a war with the United States?

We made several trips back and forth to the docks that morning to get all the barges unloaded before the bombing started. We really hustled. Afraid of being bombed and killed, we worked even harder, trying to keep our fear under control.

Around one o'clock in the afternoon we heard the first air raid sirens sounding off on Corregidor in Manila Bay. We all raced to the clearing at Little Baguio, from which we could see all the way across the bay to Manila.

We watched the Japanese planes coming in neat V formations as they flew over the city. First the bombs hit Nichols Field, and then a formation of planes hit Cavite Naval Station. As they flew past us, they dropped bombs on Corregidor. When the anti-aircraft shells exploded, it blew one of the Jap plane to bits before our very eyes. We were excited about that and cheered for our side. We looked at each other as we realized that the war really *had* started, and that we were part of it!

We went back to our camp as the all clear sounded. We were waiting for further orders and, at the same time, wondering why our P-40 fighters were not in the air engaging the Japs. And where the heck were the B-17s? What was happening? The Jap planes flew around like they owned the place, with no interference from our side.

Our group was wondering out loud about all these things. Some of the guys were ready to go back to Manila and hunt down all the Japs to kill them. As the day went on, we watched again as more waves of bombers hit Clark Field, Subic Bay, Nichols Field, Cavite Naval Station, and Corregidor. We weren't sure what other targets had been hit, but we knew—with the Japanese flying around wherever they wanted, and with no opposition—we were in deep trouble.

Sergeant Debouch came and picked out about thirty-six of us as a special convoy to take bombs to Nichols Field on the other side of Manila from where we were based. We were told that if another air attack began, we were to break up the convoy and each truck was to find its own way to Nichols Field. That way, some of us might get through; a single truck was a harder target to hit than a whole convoy.

We loaded our trucks. Each truck flew the red flag that meant we had full priority over all other traffic on the road, and each of them had a relief driver and a guard on top armed with a BAR (Browning Automatic Rifle) to look out for planes and handle any other problems that might come up. Our orders were to drive faster than normal and in close order, and not to allow any other cars or trucks between us. When we arrived in Manila, we were not to stop at any red lights, but were to flash our lights, blow horns, and keep moving, even if an air raid was in progress.

As we went through the villages where we normally traveled, the kids were out. Everyone was yelling and waving victory signs at us. They could not understand why we didn't stop at places where we would take breaks before.

As we approached Manila, we heard the air raid sirens going. We closed up our ranks even tighter and drove on. Anti-aircraft shells were exploding overhead. We could hear screams, sounds of people running, and whistles blowing. The war was on. The Filipinos were going wild.

At Nichols Field, the gate guards had problems getting us cleared to go in. We argued that we needed to get in and out before another raid. Around midnight we finally got onto the base and were told where to go to unload. Before we could get unloaded and off the base, another air raid alarm sounded. Each truck went to the back side of the field and waited. The Japanese planes came in and hit some of the hangers and a runway just a short distance from where we were. I now knew how a bomb sounded coming down toward you and how it shook the ground as it hit. My heart would almost stop as I held my breath until the bomb exploded on target. When I heard that awful thud against the target and the noise rebounding off the ground, I knew at least that I was alive for a while longer. I must have been praying, but I can't remember anything except watching the destruction all around me. I could not make myself believe this was really happening.

I saw some of our planes that had been destroyed in an earlier bombing. I couldn't figure out why they had just let them sit there and get hit. We had been warned that the Japs were coming; in fact, it was hours after we heard about Pearl Harbor that the Japanese bombs hit the Philippine Islands.

"Why were we hit like sitting ducks just waiting for it to happen?" I asked over and over. No one knew the answer.

As the all clear sounded we rolled out and went to our company compound. We found it locked up tight, as all bases were in high security mode. As we pulled into our motor pool area the air raid sirens went off again. We made it to our company quarters, where we had .50 caliber machine guns on top of the wall. As the planes flew far above us we could hear the machine guns going off. Tracer bullets formed red streaks everywhere.

When we ran out in the courtyard we could see one of our men on top of the wall. He was rocking from side to side holding our .50 caliber machine gun. His bullets were going over the river, over the top of buildings, into our quarters and compound and down the street. It was obvious he could not control where the shots were going. Sergeant Smith had to climb up the ladder and knock him off the wall to get him to stop shooting. The results of his actions were worse than those caused by the Jap bombers.

Now it was 3:30 a.m. No one in our group had rested or had any sleep since the night before. Our master sergeant made us some food. The next morning I woke up early to find that Nelda was downstairs waiting for me. I was also told that this would be the last time she could come to the compound. No visitors would be allowed from this point on, and all leaves were canceled.

When I got downstairs Nelda had been told about these rules, and she was crying. When I walked up to her she grabbed me, crying as hard as she could and holding on to me telling me how much she loved me and that she was going with me. Sergeant Warren had to pull her away from me and ask her to leave. She was yelling that I didn't know how much she loved me, so I had to promise I would come to see her. When she left I knew I might never see her again. I had never had anyone care about me like Nelda, and it was hard for me to understand her love.

WE GOT OUR ORDERS to go back to Bataan, but first we had to go to Fort William McKinley and load supplies to take with us. All of Manila was in disarray, but our company was very well organized. There were eighteen of our men in the brig when the war started, and our commanding officer told Sergeant Warren to go down and get them out because we needed them now.

I could sense special feelings towards some of us by Sgt. Warren and Sgt. Debouch, and also a very friendly attitude towards us by our officers that had not been there much before. The seven of us who had come over from the States together had been accepted into the company, and our friends and co-workers respected us for the job we were doing. Most of us were not heavy drinkers and were reliable at work.

By the time the war began in the Philippines, I had made corporal because I was going to school, which helped, but ranks in our company were slow to achieve because someone had to retire or go back to the States before anyone could be promoted. All these restrictions were gone now that the war was on; there was no retirement or returning to the States for any of us.

We went to load our trucks and try to get back to Bataan as quickly as possible. Our trip was long, but nothing much happened except a couple more air raids. It made my blood boil when I saw bombed-out houses. Once I saw a baby blown up into a tree. The island paradise that we had enjoyed had turned into a living hell for the people who lived there. They didn't know what to expect. They were all trying to be helpful, but what could they do? This was war. Rumors were going wild: "The Japs had taken Hawaii and were going to invade the U.S. west coast. They had landed north of LA." Many things were being said that confused everyone.

As soon as we got to Bataan we were told that we were not to have anything to do with anyone we didn't know, that we were not to tell where we were based or anything about our operation. Nothing. Sealed lips. We were told that the war plans called for all U.S. troops to retreat to Bataan to make their stand, if necessary.

Thirty-two men were picked to help set up field depots as close to the front lines as possible and keep them supplied with ammunition. We were also expected to supply the air bases with bombs and other ammo as needed. We were given instructions on how to build a secure ammo dump and how to dispose of it in case the ammo couldn't be removed before a retreat had to be made.

There were rumors that the Japanese were going to land troops the next day. Such rumors swirled around us constantly, but no one could tell us for sure what was happening. Though we tried not to show it, we were depressed and afraid at heart.

In the meantime the air raids had become regular occurrences. Soon we could figure out where the bombs would go and when and where to hide in case of a raid. Then we would look up at the planes passing over, knowing they would hit the main targets instead of us. They came into Clark Field while we were still there waiting to unload and dropped their bombs. Some bombs exploded within ten feet of us. The falling flack from the anti-aircraft shells being shot was just as bad or worse. It made my gut hurt that I had to lie there knowing I could do nothing except try to keep my truck, the ammo, the crew, and myself alive.

The air units were so confused that we were unable to find any-one who could tell us where to unload the 500 lb. bombs. I figured that as soon as the all clear sounded, we would dump them close to a hangar that was not too damaged. The bombs were so heavy, we needed special equipment to unload them, but there was none to be found. We decided that each truck would just let the tailgate down and then back up as fast as possible. As the driver slammed on the brakes, the bombs would roll out on the ground, with some bombs right on top of the others. We ended up putting the boxes of fuses on top of the pile of bombs. This "fast unload" process allowed us to leave before another bombing raid came over.

On our way back to Bataan we were caught by two Jap dive bomb-ers. They came in behind us. Luckily, we were close to a large, wood-ed area. We immediately drove into the jungle and were able to get all but two trucks off the road into the woods. All the trucks were emp-ty, but some were hit by bombs a few times. The two trucks that were not under cover of the trees were damaged badly, and we had to leave one truck behind.

The planes kept coming back as we moved the trucks around. None of the men were hurt, but it sure scared everyone. It was the beginning of the attacks against the ammo trucks by the dive-bombing planes. We were one of their prime targets. In spite of this, of the thirty-two men that we started with only three asked to be relieved of duty on this trip.

BEING RAISED IN A religious home, I knew what was right and what was wrong. Sometimes my upbringing made me wonder how I was going to kill anyone on purpose, but after seeing how the Japanese had bombed the people in Manila and especially seeing that little baby blown into a tree, my anger was pushed to the limit. For the first time I could see how men reacted under pressure. Their reactions made me understand that if I expected to get through this mess, I would have to kill when the time came without giving the action any thought or feeling any regret.

About the time of the second air raid in Bataan, we had noticed that when planes were approaching, the monkeys would start running and screaming in the trees. Sgt. Mahoney, our mess sergeant, was sitting at a table and heard a monkey screaming. When he looked up, a small monkey jumped up on the table, where he sat shaking and squeaking. When the bombs hit Corregidor, the monkey ran under a chair and hid there, yelling.

The little monkey took up with us later. He could tell when the planes coming over were Japanese planes. A few of our P-40s would fly over, and he would be OK, but when the Japanese planes came, he would start to sound the alarm and even beat you to the foxhole. We called him "Air-Raid Clock." He stayed with us until we had to surrender to the Japs.

OUR CREW OF THIRTY-TWO was down to twenty-nine now. The rumors were still going wild. Col. Hurst called us into a meeting to tell us what he expected of us as a working unit on the advanced ammo dumps. We were to report all air raids against the trucks and not to put any man at risk to save equipment. He told us how important it was to position an ammo dump so that aircraft could not see it. It was also important, he told us, that the supplies could be moved easily in case the lines moved back or changed.

If we had to get help at any time from the natives or other persons, we were given work slips to pay for the labor, which were backed by the U.S. government. If for any reason a man was wounded, we were to try to get him to the nearest medical corps unit. If anyone was killed, he suggested we bring their body back to the field hospital, or if we had to leave the body make a record of where the body had been left, time of death and any other information.

If for any reason we had to have transportation to return to headquarters, we were to take any car or truck we could find and give the owner a voucher so they could collect compensation from the U.S. government. In particular, we were not to tell anything to anyone about our unit or where the headquarters was located. No one was to stop us from going where we were ordered to go, regardless of his rank. We were to tell them to contact Col. Hurst at 75th Ordinance Co. to confirm our orders.

The Japanese were stepping up the number of air raids all over the place, and there were reports of their naval ships just off the coast. Expected landings were to take place any day. We had reports of small Japanese landing forces in several places on northern Luzon Island. Where were our P-40s? Why didn't they try to stop these formations of Jap bombers? That was still the big question. We didn't know that virtually all of our interceptors had been destroyed on the first day.

We were now in the second week of air attacks on all major airfields, army posts, and naval stations, and our trucks were under heavy attack every day. Our loss was small, but the guys were becoming afraid to go out during the day so most of our trips to Manila were at night. By the end of the third week our group was down to two men, Gerald Block and myself. Some refused to go out, and a couple joined units at the front line, and we never heard from them again.

THE ENGINEERS WERE ORDERED to paint all cars, trucks and equipment green—G.I. olive drab. They were to stop traffic and paint any car on the road, including windows and anything else on the vehicle that would shine or reflect light. A navy captain came to General Wainwright's headquarters with a 1942 black Buick Roadmaster that had just come in from the States. The car was pretty and shiny and probably still smelled new inside. The captain went into the headquarters building for a while. When he came out he could not find his nice black Buick anywhere. A sergeant for the engineers company was standing there, so the captain went up to him and asked, "Where is my Buick car? I left it out here."

"It's over there, Captain," replied the sergeant, pointing to some army trucks and cars. "Right where you left it, Sir."

"I don't see it, Sergeant," was his reply. The sergeant said, "It's there all right." At that point the captain saw what looked like a Buick automobile. He also realized his car was now G.I. green.

"On whose orders did you do this to my new car?" the captain shouted angrily

"Orders from USAFFE Headquarters, Sir."

The captain rushed back into General Wainwright's headquarters. There were loud words heard coming from the building. Soon the captain came out. No sooner had he come out than he rushed back in again coming out again screaming about how could they do such a thing to his nice, new Buick. When he got close to the car he realized his windshield, windows, headlights, shiny chrome and whitewall tires were all painted the GI green color, too. As he sped out of the drive he was holding the door open to see the road. His car slung gravel all over the place.

The sergeant turned around to see a small crowd watching all this action happening. All he said to the spectators was, "Just following orders. You can't please everyone."

THE FILIPINO PEOPLE WERE trying to cope with the loss of life and property due to the air raids and bracing for the Japanese invasion they knew was coming. About the 20th of December, Jap ships were offshore. They were making plans to attack our main force at Lingayen Bay. The few aircraft we had left attempted to hit the invasion force but did little damage. If our planes had been in the air on the 8th of December instead of on the ground, the invasion of the 14th Japanese Army could have been delayed or even entirely prevented. Our B-17 fleet could have taken off shortly after we were told Pearl Harbor had been hit and bombed the Japanese planes on the ground on Formosa, from where they took off.

When the 14th Japanese Army came ashore at Lingayen Bay, they were met by Filipino Army troops who were poorly trained and equipped. It was an easy landing for the Japanese forces. In some locations there was no resistance at all. I arrived near the front on the third day after the invasion to set up an ammo dump. Someone had loaded blank ammo from Fort William McKinley, not knowing the difference, and now, over eighty percent of the Filipino Army men were shooting it.

By the time we had a small ammo dump set up, the Japs were too close for us even to try to blow it up and keep it from them. I was lucky to get my crew and empty trucks out before the area was overrun. Miles down the road, I would see Filipino Army men walking away from the action. When we stopped to ask where the rest of their company was, most of the men answered that they didn't know.

As the Japs moved south quickly, USAFFE gave orders to move back into Bataan. The attempt to retreat was a total disaster. There was only one main road, and it was jammed bumper to bumper. Our troops and equipment were like sitting ducks for the Jap planes, which had a field day. A statement that came out of USAFFE said that the delay to order withdrawal back into Bataan had been caused by General MacArthur waiting to see what the intentions of the invading Japanese forces were. Believe me, when the Japanese 14th Army, one of their best, had landed and was moving fast toward Manila, it did not take a military genius to figure out what their intentions were.

The road into Bataan was closed by the Japs on the first or second of January, 1942, cutting off many Americans, Philippine scouts, and the Philippine Army, not to mention food, medical supplies, and equipment. The USAFFE had forbidden the tons of food on hand be moved to Bataan. Then, the USAFFE allowed over 30,000 old men, women and children, who were depending on the army to feed them, to move back into Bataan, where there would soon be little or nothing to eat.

General MacArthur notified Washington that the retreat was "complete and successful." The truth was that we were short on rations from the very beginning. Every living thing around—monkeys, armadillos, cats and dogs, even grubs—that could be eaten was killed by the men on Bataan and used for food.

As the first line of defense was drawn up by the Americans and Philippines, the Japanese came upon stiff resistance by the forces under General Wainwright's command. We knew it was going to get harder to hold them off, and as the overwhelming Jap forces came against us, turning our flanks, we were forced to move back farther again and again, until we were finally back as far as we could go.

THE DETAIL TO SET up ammo dumps close to the front lines was reduced to only two men out of our original thirty-two. These two men were my working partner, Gerald, and me. We lost the guards that rode on top of all trucks, and had to depend on Filipino men we were able to pick up on our way to help unload at the dumps. Many times we had to do it alone, or with the help of the army units close to the front lines.

We found ourselves between the battle lines at least twenty times, and had to fight our own way out. Our ammo dumps had been wired to blow up at the time we set them up. When we saw that we were going to lose a dump, I would order all drivers and helpers back. Gerald and I would lie in wait until the Japs were on the dump looking at their captured supplies, then we would blow the dump and them to kingdom come.

In one instance, we had five railroad boxcars half loaded with 155 black powder containers used as charges in the big guns. We waited in the bushes until about fifty Jap soldiers were all over the boxcars, checking out the contents. When we blew up the five boxcars, the Jap soldiers were blown as high as fifty to sixty feet in the air, killing all that were on the boxcars and delaying their advance. A blast of machine gun fire came our way, but fortunately we were not hit.

I WAS ON MY WAY back from the west front on January 23, 1942, when the Japanese made a push where the front was closest to the central mountain. They had also sent a landing party to the end of the Bataan Peninsula. The fight that took place there was named the "Battle of the Points." The Japs' original plan was to take Bataan by the first of February 1942, and they were right on schedule.

I was driving along the road around the southwest end of Bataan when I saw a United States major beside the road waving his arms for me to stop, so I pulled over. He said that he knew that we were an ordinance detail by the look of our trucks and wanted to know what we had on board that would help him and his small force get the Japanese who had landed below his position on the beach at Agloloma Point. All he had, he said, were rifles and a navy anti-aircraft gun that was set at a 90-degree upward angle to shoot at aircraft. They had tried to tie it to a tree to shoot down off the bluff that surrounded the beach and onto the Japs below. Each time they would shoot it though, the recoil would knock the gun off the tree and they would have to start all over again.

There were an estimated 6,000 enemy troops down there, and if we didn't do something, the major said, they would soon climb the bluff, take the highway and cut off communications between the eastern and western sides of our defense perimeter.

I asked the major where he came from in the USA, and he told me, Kansas. I asked if he knew what a hog watering or feeding trough was

"What the hell does that have to do with this situation?" he asked.

I told him we had three warehouses full of 30 lb. fragmentation bombs that we could slide down on the Japanese beachhead using the same v-shaped through-like structures that we used to slop the hogs back home. The troughs would extend out over the edge of the bluff with one end next to a tree so that we could tie off the arming wire to set the fuse when we slid the bombs down the chutes. The other end would extend out over the Japs.

He told me to go get the bombs and that they would build the chutes. I went to headquarters and talked to Col. Hurst, outlining my plan. Colonel Hurst OK'ed my idea, so I loaded up three truckloads of bombs, fuses, and arming wires and hustled back to Agloloma Point. When I got there they had seventeen chutes ready to slide the bombs down onto the Japanese beachhead, and we went to work. Some bombs hit rocks, weeds, and tree limbs, but even then the rocks rained down on the forces below. By the time we had used up two truckloads of bombs we could no longer hear any sounds coming up from below. After a little waiting time, we decided to go ahead and dump the rest of the three truckloads down on them. We killed most of them. From their own records, they said that the beachhead attempt completely failed.

I later read the following passage in official accounts of the Bataan campaign: "General MacArthur's G-2, on a staff visit to I Corps . . . became involved in [the Battle of the Points]. When all United States officers become casualties, he took command of the 1st Philippine Constabulary, defending Agloloma Point and reestablished the position by a sharp counterattack." When I read this I realized that the writer was talking about the major, me, my hog troughs and three truckloads of jerry-rigged fragmentation bombs. I have often wondered if that major was the visiting G-2 from headquarters.

Some Japs did get up the side of the bluff. The Philippine Army and other Americans that were there went hand-to-hand with them. I was walking down to one end of the bluff to see how things were going when a Jap soldier jumped out in front of me. They didn't like to shoot at close range because they would give away their location; they were supposed to use their bayonets. He lunged at me before I could get my gun into position. I stepped aside from his bayonet, but it caught my rifle strap holder and knocked my rifle out of my hand. He was just about beside me. I grabbed him around the neck and pulled out the knife that Nelda's brother had made for me. I stuck it all the way through him, nicking my own chest. I threw his body over the side of the bluff with the thought that just in case he was not dead, the drop of about 400 feet would finish him off.

As the fighting died down I could not find the major again, so I took the guys who had come with me to help unload—two Filipinos—and went back to our headquarters. I told Colonel Hurst all about our bombings and the fight. He said that we might have managed to save Bataan until the long-promised reinforcements could arrive. He called his administrative officer, Major Potter, and told him to put me down to receive the Medal of Honor for my action. This was the first defeat the Japs had suffered since they started the war. The Battle of the Points, as it was called, gave Bataan two more months to wait for help. I consider this one of the most important engagements in the Pacific at that time.

The time it took Japan to pull back some of its forces from the South Pacific helped save Australia from invasion, shortening the war by a year. If the attempted Japanese landing had been successful, their push on land on our west flank would have linked up with the Algoloma Point landing. This would have cut our supply line to the west front, and Bataan would have fallen within a few days. Then the Japanese would only have had Corregidor to take and the Philippine campaign would have been complete, because in the end, Corregidor only held up twenty-three days after Bataan fell. Mac Arthur would not have made it to Australia and would have been captured.

When it got down to the facts of holding Bataan, the job was to fight with no restrictions. The officers and men showed what they were made of and the spirit they had to hold off the forces that vastly outnumbered them from the very beginning. General McArthur passed command to General Wainwright, who had little to work with. Pushed back against the China Sea with orders to fight to the last man, what could he do except pick up whatever pieces were left?

THE PROPAGANDA FROM THE radio station finally stopped. We were no longer expecting anything from anyone. General King—who I think was a great general—was faced with a bigger problem. He had inherited an order to do the impossible, hold off longer at a great cost of life, or decide just when and how to get out of this dilemma. The facts were right there before him. He was faced with the starving civilians in a camp that was formed for the women and children caught up in the retreat back to Bataan. The soldiers who were trying to fight were sick and worn out from the horrors of war. The front line smelled from one end to the other with the stench of dead men. Jap bodies lay everywhere. No one wanted to bury them. Getting the wounded back to a corpsman so they could be taken to the hospital was almost impossible. Some wounded were never moved from where they fell, because the fighting would not permit it.

During this time, I scarcely had a chance to visit Nelda in the civilian camp and help her however I could. Every minute of my time was consumed with getting needed ammo to the men. Nelda, too, was getting desperate for food the same as the others in the camp. Although she thought she could be of help to others, she was restricted as to where she could go. When I looked at the women and children, I knew that the same questions were on their minds: "Will we be safe here? Is any help coming?" As in other places, optimistic rumors proved to be false.

There was not much time to think about home or tomorrow just now. I was just barely holding onto life and body. When I had time to think, my thoughts would drift to my family and girl back home and wonder if I would ever make it back there, myself. I guess that's when hope started to enter my mind. Sometimes I would think about places and the things I had done, especially where there was a question as to whether I had done right or wrong.

SOMETIMES ANGER TAKES THE place of reasoning, as it did when I was on the front line and the fighting was ferocious. The Philippine Army had captured about forty Jap soldiers. Gerald and I were the only Americans present. They asked us what to do with them. I said to the sergeant in charge, "Are you going to feed them or take care of them?"

He looked back at me and said, "That's what I want you to do, take them back to a prison camp. I do not know of one."

My suggestion was that since food was so short, he could take them down the road a ways and let them escape. I asked him if he knew what to do when prisoners tried to escape. The sergeant smiled and made his men march the Japs down the road. Soon we heard shots, and when they came back he looked at me and told me the prisoners tried to escape.

Our orders were not to stop the ammo truck for anything and to keep rolling. One night there was a big wreck involving an ambulance going back to the hospital with wounded men. When I stopped to look, I could see a man I knew. His name was Jolly, and the ambulance was lying on his arm. We took the truck winch and lifted the wrecked ambulance to release him. I understand that he lost his arm, but at least he did not lie there and bleed to death.

On another occasion we were told to go to a certain point on the front, but when we got there the place had already fallen into Japanese hands. Before we knew it, our trucks were surrounded by Japs. There were six trucks. My truck was the lead truck and Gerald's was in the rear. The Corbitt trucks had loud air horns. When I saw what was happening, I blew the horn, the next one blew his horn and so on down the line.

The loud noise of the truck horns stunned the Japs for a moment. I bailed out of my truck and ran back. The other trucks started backing up. The Japs started shooting and the relief drivers started returning the fire. I jumped on the side of the second truck. Our plan worked great. Each truck turned at the same time except Gerald's. He started shooting at the truck I had just abandoned. It was loaded with 155 big gun black powder charges. When he hit those canisters, the truck blew to pieces. One of our relief drivers was killed and we lost the truck I was driving, but at least we got out of there.

The explosion of my truck gave us time to back down the road. About three miles back we saw the Philippine Army unit we were looking for. We told the lieutenant in charge to always give us a signal if they retreated. Their ammo was short and the Japs were moving in from the side, so they had to get out with their big gun as quickly as they could because the front line had collapsed without their knowledge. The big gun was about ten miles down the road behind us by that time. There were so few of the big 155s that we did everything we could to save them.

A request for repairing a 155 gun came in from a front line Philippine scouting company close to the front lines. The company was located on a mountain point close to a road intersection that was the command post overlooking the valley where the Japs were advancing. It was a must to save that gun and the command lookout, too, if possible. By the time Gerald and I arrived at the location, the top of the hill had changed hands three times. We had the parts to fix the gun but we had to wait for the Philippine scouts to take back the top of the mountain so we could get down the road to where the big gun was located.

Heavy fighting raged all night. By daybreak there was a lull, and we got word to move out. I was driving the big Corbitt truck with the big gun in tow. Gerald and I were prepared. Four BARs were loaded with 30 round clips. In addition to the BARs, we had three or four Springfield rifles and our .45 pistols, plus dozens of hand grenades. Our windshield was opened out. All the windows were down. We were warned that the Japs were close to the intersection.

As we approached the three-road intersection, there in front of us was a Jap setting up a tripod machine gun. Gerald took a BAR and emptied the 30-round clip into the Jap, just blowing him to pieces. As this happened, we were turning right to go down the mountain road, which had five switchback curves. The Philippine troops were on the right side of the road, and the Japs were on the left. We found ourselves taking heavy gunfire from both sides.

Gerald yelled that a Jap soldier was in the middle of the road. Gerald fired and the Jap jumped in the ditch. I had the truck accelerator to the floor. The first curve was an inside curve, and as I looked at the side mirror I could see the long gun barrel scraping the inside bank of the mountain. On the next curve the wheels of the trailer were half off the side of the mountain. The Jap who was in the road was in the next inside curve. The gun barrel got him as he tried to get away.

Gunshots were so close you could feel the concussion against your ears. We went down and around the next two zigzag curves at full speed. As we leveled off at the bottom, we saw the Philippine scout's checkpoint where we were to leave the gun.

I thought the gas pedal was stuck until Gerald kicked my foot off of it. I was frozen to the accelerator with only one thought in mind—to get down the mountain and get the gun in place. As we came to a stop, the scouts were chasing us to get the gun. When we got out of the truck we counted thirty-two bullet holes in the cab. Neither Gerald nor I had one scratch on us. I have said the angels had been there to protect us. When we arrived back at headquarters, no one could believe we were in that truck and survived when it had been shot so many times.

One night I was returning with our crew and a convoy of about eight trucks. I was the lead truck. We were in the foothills, and there was a drop of about 300 feet on the outside of the road. As I came into a curve, a jeep came around the curve toward us at a great rate of speed. I had the truck door open with one foot on the running board and the other on the gas pedal. In trying to miss the jeep, my left front wheel hit a washout on the side of the road and my truck flipped over. The door served as a lever that threw the truck over the side of the mountain down 300 feet. I fell out and that truck flipped right over me, leaving me at the edge of the bluff without a scratch.

Jap snipers would often get behind our lines. They would try to place themselves in a tree so they could see as much of the road as possible, then sit there waiting for something important to come by. Our ammo trucks were always considered a top target, so we were always watching for the snipers. Many times they would shoot out a windshield or kill one of our drivers.

A 155 big gun on our west China Sea front needed a part. I took a jeep and a Filipino relief driver with me to go repair the gun. When we had to deliver anything like this we flew a big red flag. Unfortunately, it was also notice to a sniper that our jeep was on an important mission.

It was late afternoon when we went around a curve. The sniper shot out our windshield with a burst of shots. I pulled the jeep into the left ditch. The ditch was so full of powder dust that it filled my nose and lungs and made it hard to get my breath. I crawled up on the bank next to the jeep to get some protection from the sniper. The Jap must have thought we were dead. All was quiet and no one came along for about fifteen minutes. Then I heard a truck coming. I crawled back in the ditch and along the ditch until I thought the sniper could not see me. I saw the truck in time to warn him that a sniper was up ahead and the driver stopped. The driver was a Filipino scout. I told him to stay there and stop anyone. He told me there were some men a short distance back down the road. He walked back and brought about six other men with him. We decided to try to find the sniper.

They gave me a Springfield rifle because I could not get safely back to my jeep. When I told them what mission I was on, they told me they must find this Jap and get me on the way. We spread out in different directions trying to pin the sniper down. It was getting dark, and we knew if we didn't get him soon, it would be too late to try.

For a little while everything was quiet, then a group of men began walking down the road toward my jeep from a different direction. A sudden burst of gunfire came from a tree toward the men walking down the road. Three of us were close to the tree where the sniper was sitting. I opened fire and so did the other two men. We could see the Jap trying to move in the tree. At that point another blast of gunfire came from the tree. That gave us his exact location. All of us seven men fired into the tree, and the sniper fell out. One of the scouts ran up to see if he was dead and got his gun.

When I returned to my jeep, my relief driver was dead. One of the men who had been walking down the road was also dead, and another had been shot in the leg.

Once while we were trapped between the lines I was hit by shell fragments in the right side. A Filipino corpsman took the piece of steel out and patched me up. There was no one to drive my truck, so I drove back to headquarters and never had time to go to the field hospital.

The troops on Bataan had their food rations cut to less than half. One can of salmon and rice was the main thing about thirty men were eating. All the horses, water buffalo, monkeys, snakes and lizards were eaten, including wild boars and anything else we could get. The iodine that was used to put into contaminated water to make it safe to drink was about gone. Malaria was rampant. When I would go to the front lines, I found that the men were hungry, their clothes ragged, their hearts broken, and their morale low.

Short wave radio would pick up the Voice of America. I can still think back and hear them saying, "Good morning, fellow Americans (or Mr. And Mrs. America). The rocky walls of Bataan still stand this morning. The battle-weary Americans and Filipino troops still hold against overwhelming odds. The full force of the powerful Imperial Japanese Army has been unable to break the lines of these brave fighting men. General McArthur expects the forces in Bataan will hold out until reinforcements arrive."

At that point we would turn to another station to hear what Tokyo Rose would say about the report from the Voice of America from San Francisco. She would say something like this, "Good morning, Boys. You know help is not on the way. Well, we have something for you today. The Imperial Japanese Army has your menu ready for you. It's time you raise your white flag and come over to us and get some clean clothes, good food, and good music. The Americans do not care about you. There is no way to win."

She would continue, "The 14th Army has this planned for you today. At dawn this morning the shelling began in the Moran area. Bombing and strafing will continue all day. Shelling will be done all up and down the front lines. Now why do you want to stay there and get killed or injured when you could be safe by simply coming across our lines? We will see that you are treated well. Now here is some music to help you remember your friends and family back home."

Now can you imagine what this did to us poor dogfaces that were nailed down, fighting a war, fighting sickness, with no food, dirty clothes and no way to wash them, having people who were safe and sound sikking the big dog on us. I felt like everyone else. Why were we here in this jam with our own people making it worse? While this was going on, the radio station on Corregidor was also putting out some mess that sure didn't help us. They did not impress the Japs because they knew how things were on Bataan. We poor suckers who were on the front lines had nothing but a blue sky overhead, not the protection of a big tunnel like most of the men on Corregidor.

THE FINAL WEEKS AND days on Bataan were brutal. Some men were so sick they could not even hold their heads up but were expected to hold the line against the Japs. Their patrols were testing our lines every time they could, day and night. The shells kept coming in.

The radio station at Corregidor sent this interview out:

Q. "Good morning, Sergeant. You look fresh this morning with nice clean clothes on. Where have you been?"

A. "Well," he said, "I've been taking it easy for a couple of weeks. You know the fighting on Bataan has slowed down and I've been over there seeing some of my friends, just lying around taking it easy."

Q. "How are conditions there? I've heard that food is short."

A. "No," the sergeant answered, "while I was over there some fresh bread arrived, and we threw the old bread out."

At that point we turned the radio off. Bull like that may have had some effect on the Japs, but not on us.

At the same time these radio shows were going on, the army radio kept telling us, "Help is on the way." One radio voice said, "I looked out the plane window and as far as I could see there were ships headed this way." Then all of a sudden we got the news that General McArthur was on his way to Australia. To us his words, "I shall return," rang hollow.

Here we were, faced with orders to fight to the last man, and he's off to get help. What a thing to tell men who knew more than anyone what the score really was. Why didn't he level with us? "Say men, we are in a mess. Our food is about gone, ammo is getting low, and things are bad. The help from America cannot get here in time. God bless you; do what you can." Our respect for the great general would have been greater.

We could remember the planes that were hit on the ground at Clark and Nichols Field, the ships that sat at Cavite Naval Base and were destroyed, and the delay in opposing the Japs when they landed at Lengayen Bay. We all remembered this as a big goof-up as far as we were concerned. We felt like the Philippine Islands were handed to the Japanese on a silver platter. You know, the buck stops at the top.

ON A RUN TO OUR western China Sea front, we were spotted by a couple of Zeroes (Japanese fighter plane) that caught us on an open road. Each truck tried to make it to a large tree for cover, but my truck was unable to get under one or hide anywhere. They were so close I didn't have time to run into the jungle, so I got out and under the motor area as a Zero came down the road strafing. For some reason he quit strafing and pulled up. His last bullet hit up front so close the dirt flew all over me under the truck. As he made his way around to come back I ran to a rice haystack and was hit in my legs by bomb fragments. Two of the pieces had to be removed at a field hospital, but there was no time off because I had to work. My legs were so bad that I would take a stick sometimes to help me push the gas pedal down.

The drivers and helpers started shooting at the plane. It started

65

smoking and fell to the ground over a small hill. One of our group went to see if the pilot was dead, and he was.

Gerald and I knew our time was getting short. Bataan could not stand another push by the Japs and hold out much longer. Everywhere you looked there were desperate men wanting to know if we had anything to eat and asking how the front line was holding. You could read desperation on all their faces. Filipinos were walking around like they were in a daze. When you asked them where they were going or where their unit was, they would just look at you and say, "They all dead, Joe. No unit. All men killed."

It was true that we killed thousands of the Japs, so many that we had a lull in the fighting for several weeks while they brought in reinforcements, but then it started picking up again. That was not a good sign. Our men were sicker, not as organized as before, and the Filipino army was about gone. The hope of holding off the Japanese was fading day by day. Back at our company headquarters, Col. Hurst was already planning to blow up all the ammo warehouses if we were taken. Gerald and I had stashed a small boat north of the airstrip at the end of Bataan and loaded it with supplies in hopes we could get out that way in case of surrender. That was our plan.

There was a Captain Little there. He was telling us if we were captured to tell the Japs only our name and service number. He said it would be better to say you were a private, because they expected the lower ranking soldiers to be dumb to an extent. So I remembered that advice. Also, we were to say we were cooks and never tell them we were with the 75th Ordinance.

Colonel Hurst had Gerald and me help with the demolition of the warehouse. We were to blow the big ammo dump, since we knew what was about to happen and that our lines could not hold out much longer. The sound of shells hitting over the west front had picked up.

The job would have to be done within the next few hours.

I took off to go see Nelda, and in effect, say goodbye, for she did not know about the boat. Gerald and I were going to try to get away on it, and there was just room enough for two. Nelda was out of control crying, for she knew what was ahead. She asked me to come back. She said she would put women's clothes on me and try to get me out with the civilians. Of course, I had to tell her I could not do that. When I left to go back to headquarters she was on the ground crying, but I knew I had to go help blow the big ammo dump.

It was getting dark by the time I got back to headquarters. We were told that General King had signed an unconditional surrender, and that we must lay down our arms and go to several spots to meet the Japs. That night we blew the top off the hill at Little Baguio. It looked like the biggest fireworks show ever. After that we were simply told to take care of ourselves, and good luck.

No one except Gerald and I knew about our attempt to get away. Gerald said he had one other thing he had to do. He ran to our pup tent and grabbed three hand grenades, then ran up hill to the hospital area. About nine Japs were being held in a small area there. I heard three explosions and he came running back down the hill with a grin on his face. He said, "They won't be eating any more of our food."

When we returned to Bataan, they had opened the Little Bagiuo Hospital just a short distance from our company area. General Wainwright's hospital was within a quarter mile of us. The next day a friend and I walked up to the Little Baguio Hospital. As we approached one of the large crosses located at one corner of the hospital, a Jap dive bomber came in low, dropped his bombs, and strafed the entire area a couple of times. One of the bombs dropped next to the white cross as if to say the pilot knew this was a hospital. I went into the ditch on the right side and my friend went into the left side of the road. As the plane turned I could see the Jap pilot look back. I could have grabbed the plane with my bare hands and crushed him to the earth.

As I looked for my friend I couldn't find him. I noticed a bomb hit on the left side where he had been. Then I saw a shoe. When I picked it up, I realized his foot was in it. That was all I could find of him. After my initial shock, I became enraged at the Jap pilots for hitting our hospitals.

That was the turning point for me. I knew right then that they did not care who or what they hit. Hatred took control of me, and I wanted to kill every Jap I could see. I think at this point my fears about dying or getting hurt were gone. I wanted first to see a Jap I could kill and then do it without any feeling at all. This day became "K" day for me: "Kill the Japs Day."

The last thing we did at our Bataan location was to take Old Glory down, putting it in a sealed tube and burying it with intention to come back and retrieve it. We would never see that flag again. All of us there had tears flowing down their faces Many times after that I thought about the men that never saw Old Glory fly again.

— 4 —

The Bataan Death March

THE FEAR OF BECOMING prisoners of war was always on our minds, and Gerald and I had discussed many schemes to avoid being captured. On one of our trips to Manila we had found a small boat that was left without an owner. It looked fairly seaworthy, but needed a little repair. We were elated at the thought of having some way to avoid being captured. After checking with the people in the area to try to find the owner of the boat, a Filipino offered it to us. We did a few quick repairs to it, and then stashed it in a remote area on the China Sea side of Bataan. We were confident we could escape the Japs by sea, if we had to.

Hearing the news that General King had surrendered the troops on Bataan, Gerald and I immediately headed over the hill to get to our boat. On the way to escape, we saw trucks being destroyed to keep the Japs from getting them. All the guns were being taken apart and thrown away, along with everything else of value.

As we made our way through the jungle we noticed a clearing on the side of the mountain. We were high above the Maravelles airstrip and had about four miles to go to reach the road we needed to cross to get to the placed where our boat was stashed. We each had a .45 caliber pistol, a BAR (Browning Automatic Rifle) and several hand grenades.

As we approached the winding road coming down the mountainside we saw a crowd of men walking and a bus loaded with Filipinos. All of them were waving Japanese flags. We couldn't believe it. Where had they gotten those flags? Gerald lifted his BAR and told me those Filipinos wouldn't be able to keep those Jap flags and started firing. The bus went off the road and plunged to the bottom of the ravine. We stood there, watching. There was no movement and no sound. We did not say a word to each other; we just started off again.

Suddenly, we heard a tank coming, by the sound of it a Japanese tank. Now we had a big problem. We had to get across the road without being seen, since there was no other way to reach our boat. We decided to lay low for a little while to see if any Japanese foot soldiers were with the tank. Sure enough, there were long columns of men following the tank going in the direction of the airstrip. Some of the soldiers were jabbing the bushes along the road with their rifles, searching for anyone trying to hide. Then we saw Americans and Filipinos with their hands in the air following close behind the formation.

"It's time to move back," I told Gerald. "If we see we are going to be captured, we must throw away our guns." Gerald told me no way was he going to throw away his gun; he planned to shoot his way out of there. He had a .32 caliber nickel-plated pistol in his backpack taken from a dead Japanese soldier. He said he was going to try to get it through the Japanese lines. We had been told not to have anything on us like guns, knives, ammo or anything we had taken off a dead Jap. It was known that if the Japanese soldiers found anything like that on you, they would shoot you on the spot. I told Gerald he had better get rid of that pistol in case we were caught crossing the road.

Gerald had a new pair of black and white shoes in his backpack that he had bought just before leaving Manila. He had worn them only a couple of times. Now he sat down and put them on.

There were more and more Japanese coming down the road, plus several trucks and tanks. Right in front of where we were hidden, they pulled off the road and started motioning others to pull over. We figured they were stopping to set up a camp. We would have to get out of the ditch we were in and go back up the hill to get across the road. We were speaking in whispers, but it was hard to hear each other because our hearts were pounding so hard.

All of a sudden we heard something behind us. When we turned around, we saw six Japs with guns and bayonets pointing at us. They were motioning for us to climb out of the ditch and to throw down our guns. Gerald slipped the .32 out of his back pocket and stuck it in a pocket of his backpack, then turned the backpack over. When he picked up the backpack, he knocked the gun out onto the grass without the soldiers seeing it. They motioned for us to go to the road and start marching. I said something to Gerald and a Jap hit me in the back of my head with his rifle and shook his head, motioning for us not to talk.

As we walked toward the road my thoughts went to Nelda, wondering if she was okay. At this point I knew my own future was uncertain. This was the lowest time in my life. Why had the army not helped us? I was so angry that I think if a newly landed American soldier had walked up to me at that moment I would have hit him. Here we were facing the very enemy we had fought to keep from taking Bataan, prisoners of war facing the Japanese, for whom I had built up so much hatred. This was the worst thing that could have happened to me. I was almost sick to my stomach with rage and despair at my helplessness to do anything about my situation.

What an empty feeling, not knowing where they would take us or what they would do with us. We had no way to defend ourselves. If only I could have had a minute to talk to God, but I had no time to pray as I walked; every minute I had to watch everything going on around me. I could see up ahead that a Jap was beating an American with his rifle. A Japanese soldier, who could speak a little English, told us that we had to meet and line up on the runway at the airstrip.

As we walked to the runway, the Japs we were with moved off to the side of the road. Another group of Jap soldiers was yelling as they pushed us into a large group of Americans. We figured this was our shakedown. Behind us was a tank with a Jap standing up in the hatch pointing a machine gun at us. Another Jap came from behind the tank, yelling at us. He was hitting and kicking most of the men and telling them to line up, step back four paces and out an arm's length from the man next to him.

We were ordered to put our backpack and everything in our pockets on the ground in front of us. When they came to you in the line, if you had anything that might have come off a Japanese soldier, you were led to the back of the line and then we would hear a shot. If you had any guns, ammo or knives, you were beaten or killed. When a Jap searched you, if he found anything in your pockets he didn't like, depending on what it was, you were beaten or shot. I was numb, watching what was going on like I was not even there. I guess I was waiting to be killed. When you are seventeen, you have a feeling you will live forever. It was a shock to find out this would not be true in my case!

There were three Japs walking the line inspecting what we had on the ground in front of us. Each one took anything he wanted—a watch, a ring—anything. They had armed guards watching everything. If you tried to move anything, they would pull you out of line and take you away. I have no clue where they took those people. We had stood there at least an hour and a half when we were told to pick up our things and move down the road. I thought it was great that they didn't take the candy I had in my backpack that had come with our C-rations. We had been hoarding things for three months, saving them for our escape attempt.

No one could ever imagine how lost we felt. We were broken in spirit and getting very hungry and thirsty walking down a dusty road to nowhere—all the while watching the obvious joy of the Japs because they had taken the Americans. While we marched, Gerald and I were looking for a place to take off into the woods without the guards seeing us. We went around a curve and saw a trail leading up into the jungle. We took it. While we were making our way up to a clearing we noticed someone over on the other side, so we turned to go through the dense jungle away from them and back toward the road.

We dived into some bushes and lay very still when a couple of Japs came by. I suppose they were looking for us. We hardly breathed as they went by, we were so afraid they might hear us. After they passed us, we started up the hill again and soon we were back on the trail. Then we heard something behind us and looked back. There were two Japs behind us. They motioned for us to go on ahead. We soon came to a small clearing and found four more Japs sitting there. The other two explained to them that we had been coming up the trail. We could not fully understand what they were saying, but could read their motions as to what they meant some of the time.

They made us take our backpacks off and lay the contents out so they could see everything. That's what they wanted. They took our watches, which hadn't been taken at the first shakedown. They also took candy, our shirts, and underclothes. They took everything. They took our water canteen and poured the water out on the ground and, to our surprise, let us go without hitting us. One followed us until we came to the road again and told us to get into the group. He said something to the other guard, then he came over and slapped both of us. We didn't know what the slap was for, but that is when I considered the Death March to have actually begun for Gerald and me.

73

IT WAS LATE AFTERNOON on the first day, April 9, 1942. Gerald and I had been stripped of most of our belongings. I had only a sun helmet, shirt, black pants, and an empty canteen hanging by a chain around my belt. Gerald had about the same things left, but he had a towel around his neck and the black and white shoes that were already hurting his feet. I figured we had already walked about thirty miles trying to get to the boat we had stashed.

In the beginning it was not so bad. The yelling, the beatings, and the shouting were expected. Now that we were in the crowd with other Americans and Filipinos, it was time to make the best of it. My dad had taught me to adjust to any circumstance as quickly as possible. This training had already saved my life several times during the fighting, but for Gerald it was not so easy. He was already fussing, whining, and complaining about things. I had to keep telling him, "Look, we have to make the best of this because we no longer have the power to change any of these things. This is a battle, and we are fighting to save our lives."

The night went as well as one could expect as we just kept marching. The next morning, trucks and equipment that had been destroyed to keep the Japs from using them lined the side of the road. The sun was now beating down on us, and at this time of year, it could get really hot. As we marched out of the mountains where more Japs were gathered, things started to change. Some of the men were slowing down. If anyone stopped, they were shot or bayoneted to death. My mind could not comprehend that these men were being brutally murdered in front of all of us.

Japanese lined the road taking pictures. Some of the men who had been sick before the march started, began to drop by the side of the road. As we passed, a few men were asking for help, but we soon found out if you tried to help them, the Japs would start shooting at you. Many men died this way.

The nights at first were bad. We were marching in columns of four. As the trucks came by the Japs in the back of the truck would stick their guns with fixed bayonets out between the wooden sides of the truck and try to hit men marching in the right column in the head with the bayonets or any other object that would cause injury. I saw several men killed that way. In spite of everything, Gerald and I managed to stay together.

The Japanese would be resting on the left side of the road. If they saw someone with a ring, watch or any other thing of value, they would take it. Most of the time if the man didn't give it willingly, he was shot or his finger cut off to get the ring.

After the first night, daylight showed we were out of the mountains. We had not stopped for anything and we needed water. We knew that there were artesian water wells along the road, so we were hopeful of getting a drink. As we approached the first well we could see men running to get water. We also saw two guards wait until they got to the water, then shoot them. There must have been at least 200 bodies around that well. Somehow water didn't seem important enough to die for, so I continued to march.

We were now coming to the first little Filipino villages. Some of the villagers were trying to throw us food. A Jap was in the village and brought a woman and a girl, who was about nine years old, out in the road at gunpoint. The woman was pregnant. The Jap cut her throat in front of her child, then he cut her stomach open as we passed. We could see her unborn child half out of her stomach. It was a gruesome sight and almost made me sick. The Jap told the girl to go back to the village. When she got to the edge of the road he shot her in the back. I had to hold Gerald back. He was ready to kill that Jap. He looked at me and said, "See what you did? You made me get rid of my .32 revolver, and I could have shot that Jap."

As we marched we could hear men screaming. Some were begging for water and food, but there was nothing you could do to help them. None of us now had anything left but the clothes on our back. The sun was hot and the road was hotter. The march and the heat were beginning to take their toll on us. Gerald and I figured we had to survive this thing. We had been in many tight spots before and had come through them.

We came to a place where the Japs took several men out of line, stopping at the man marching in front of me. As we marched on, we could see what they were doing with them. There was a bomb crater in the road, and these men were being made to shovel dirt into this hole, which was half full of water.

As we passed close by, I could see the Japs kicking men who could no longer lift their shovels into the hole. A couple of soldiers on the bank with long bamboo poles were pushing them under the water and mud. They were being buried alive. Seeing that quickly made us change the lines we marched in. As the marchers got a little scattered, we took our positions in the third column on the road. This gave us two men to our right and one to the outside of the road next to the ditch.

Now the men were dropping like flies. A convoy of Japanese trucks was coming. When a body fell into the road, the first truck driver would see it and swerve his truck to run over it. The crunch of breaking bones made me want to throw up. The following trucks would do the same. The body was pounded into the road like a dead dog—just another thing that added to the rage of hate flowing through us.

No food or water, and the march kept on. No sleep for us, as we were not allowed to stop. You could see water, but were forbidden to drink. The Japs were stopped along the road with their canteens, eating their rations. The feeling of hunger was slowly leaving me, but it was a terrible thing to see them eating when they would not feed us anything. What were they going to do with us?

Most of the men with us were American. We were not sure how the Filipino soldiers were making out. My whole body was aching, and I craved water.

BY THE SECOND DAY, the reality of defeat had finally sunk into my mind. While I walked it was time to take stock and think about the reality of being a prisoner of war. Never in my wildest dreams could I have imagined the events of the past few days. The unbelievable had happened. The fight was over. The Japs had won. I was in a group of men marching in columns of four down a road that I had traveled so many times with big red flags flying on the front of my truck, having priority over the use of the road. Everything or everyone had to yield to us as we drove the big trucks furnishing ammo to the front lines. Then I realized there were no more front lines, no more fighting for our country. Now I was fighting for my own life.

The feelings I had during the last days of the fighting made me think how true Tokyo Rose's words had been. Her words would ring like an alarm clock to wake you up. She was right, there had been no reinforcements. MacArthur was a liar. All his promises were just wishful thinking.

The men who fought on Bataan were like no others in the history of America. They served in honor and fought way beyond the call of duty. So many of them gave their lives—for what? Now we were subject to brutal acts by an army of barbaric Japanese Imperial troops who took pleasure in blatant murder, using their bayonets and sabers to slice us up as if we were mad dogs.

As I put one foot ahead of another, I wondered why my life had not been taken during the fighting, even if my body were left to decay, to return to God in the same manner that I came—ashes to ashes, dust to dust. At least a death while fighting would have been an honorable death. Now, all that mattered was what I could make of this present situation. There was no one who could halfway understand what was happening to us.

As I looked around at all the bodies along the road, the sight made me realize that this was going to be another kind of killing field, totally unlike that of battle. This time we were like sitting ducks, stripped of our honor, our guns, and most of all, our ability to defend ourselves against such acts of horror.

My thoughts raced back home. How lucky I was to still be alive—or was I lucky at all? But these thoughts made me realize that I had to figure out a way to survive this terrible ordeal if I wanted to live long enough to return home. Then suddenly the will to survive came over me, and I knew I had the pure guts to make it.

THE MORNING AIR MOVED slowly along the jungle trees, and at times the stench of death was unbearable. This smell only served to remind me of the men I had killed and the men the Japanese were killing now. The only satisfaction I had was the thought that it was their time now, and it had been my time for the past four months. To think I was any different from any other man who had given his life made no sense to me. When I looked up, I could see the vultures flying around. I thought about how wonderful it would be to be one of them, to be able to just fly away or to find a good meal. There was plenty around to feed them. For us there was no food. Maybe God had thought of everything. One creature's death gave life to another. The Japs were having their heyday. The victory was theirs, and the loss was ours.

Once in awhile I would look around to see if my friend Gerald was still there, knowing that if he needed help it would be impossible to give it to him. I'm sure he felt the same about me. We had stood side by side through so many close calls. At least the Japanese could have given those of us who were dying a last chance to live, but no, these soldiers took pleasure in killing. Even innocent Filipino people who happened to get in their way were killed for no reason at all.

As I put one foot in front of another my anger continued to grow, but I knew that there was nothing I could do to change what was happening, because I would only end up as another dead American to lie unnoticed. What good would it do at this point to make an effort when nothing would change? I knew I had to accept these acts of murder, had to pick up my feet and push forward so I would not incur the wrath of these ruthless savages. I was proud of the times that I had not given the Japs a chance to live when I had the upper hand.

We had to push on as far as our bodies would take us in hopes we would make the finish line, wherever that was, or whenever this terrible march would be over. At that point I was determined that they would have a hard time killing me, for I would not break for water or do anything to bring a Jap guard's attention my way. I accepted my fate and adjusted quickly to conditions at hand, with my mind made up that they could not kill me until I had exhausted every effort in my body and soul to meet whatever was ahead.

Seeing death all around was nothing new to us by now, and the feeling would cross my mind that maybe dying would be an easy way out, but I was not ready to accept that fate at this point. So I told myself to forget about the hunger, forget about the thirst, forget about the pain, forget about the killing, and push on step by step. Just let my body become as numb as possible. Don't think. Don't feel. Just keep moving.

On the third day the steps were harder to take. The bayonet killings and the beatings were taking more lives. I tried not to notice. My mind was taking me in the same direction as I think the Japs' minds were going. If I could have changed places for a while I would have killed them all, just as I saw them kill Americans and Filipinos. My heart had grown harder. Maybe I could live to pay them back with the same treatment they had imposed on us.

As the sun rose we could see more horrible things from the night before that added to the feeling that it was only a matter of time before each of us would be among the dead. The hunger and thirst was not as bad as the day before, but I could tell that my once strong, young body was feeling the effect of this endless ordeal.

On the fourth day, as the sun rose again to show us what was happening around us, the stench of death was even worse than before. The sun seemed to be hotter, my steps harder to take. My body and mind were playing tricks on me. My legs seemed to swell and my feet didn't feel like feet anymore. My legs and joints were getting harder to move, but I had to go forward at all costs.

I thought about what Gerald had said, "Wait until we are out of Bataan, then make a break to escape." But now escape would be impossible because there was no one who could help us. Our legs would not stand any attempt to run. When I looked at Gerald his face showed the strain, and I'm sure he felt a great deal of pain. During the night some men in our group had started singing the Star Spangled Banner and shortly afterwards a machine gun burst must have killed at least fifty to a hundred of us.

We were moving out of the old war zone to where some Filipino people were standing. They tried to throw us sugar cakes, but the guards opened fire on them. At least six of them were killed. Then the guards went into their houses yelling and shooting everyone in the house. Some of them ran. I saw a young Filipino woman killed with a saber.

It was now the fifth day. Our ranks were thinning out. I began to wonder how it would feel when my eyes would no longer stay open. Would I fall asleep as I walked? Gerald and I were in the third column from the road. We were going to try to make it to a ditch if either of us could not manage to stay standing up. We planned to try to hide and take our chances until night in hopes we could get some rest, then get back in line the next morning. But for now we were still on our feet and marching steadily forward. Gerald's new black and white shoes had his feet in blisters and open cuts, but his will was like steel. If anyone could make it, he could. But how much longer could each of us hold out? Now the thought of food and water did not worry me as much as the pain in my legs and feet.

On the night between the fifth and sixth days, it rained. The water that one could catch in his hand helped. I turned my head up and opened my mouth to catch a little water. The guards could not see us. I think it was an act of God that we got that little bit of water. Gerald sucked a little of it out of the dirty towel he had around his neck, and that helped him. The guards' yelling and killing was no different than before, but we had accepted it as part of what we had to face. We were still determined to take everything dished out to us until we had finished this march.

On the seventh night we were all so weak that picking up our feet was out of the question. Al we could do was shuffle along. There were far fewer of us now, and sometimes there were fifty feet of space between the guy ahead of me and my place in line. I had lost sight of Gerald. I knew he was somewhere around me, but I could no longer worry about it. I could hear my feet dragging, but was unable to pick them up. No longer could I think about anything except trying to keep from falling, because that would be a sure death. I also would get the feeling that maybe I should just drop to the ground and take a shot or a bayonet to end it all. But for some reason a flare of hope would come over me, and I knew I had to keep sliding my feet and not accept defeat.

Soon the ranks started closing up again. Everyone was moving more and more slowly. As I looked up I could see they were letting us go into a fenced in area. Some men were stopped and some were falling down, but no guns were shooting. I thought, God help us if this is not the end. Soon I was jammed up against someone else. We were very close to each other. He said we are going to get some rest. Let's all slide down on the ground. There was nowhere to fall, so we would just jam our body between others. Your feet and legs were someplace, but it did not seem to matter. I think I was asleep before my body touched the ground.

We were in a holding pen at San Fernando. Some time later a blast of machine gun fire caused a rush to one side of the compound. When I looked around I saw that the holding pen was partly empty except for some bodies that didn't move. The rush must have been an automatic reflex. I had no idea where Gerald was, but did not see his body on the ground in the morning when they made us load into small railroad cars. They loaded as many as they could pack into a car, beating the ones who had trouble moving. Everyone there was slow to move, so it was hard to tell which ones they were going to beat.

Then they closed the doors of the railroad cars. The only air we had was from the small holes in the sides of the cars. We must have sat there for a couple of hours. As the sun rose higher, the cars got very hot. It was a great relief when the train started to move out. We had ridden for about an hour before we stopped and the doors were opened. In the car I was in, many were dead. The Japanese guards kicked and rolled their bodies out onto the ground, yelling and beating as many of us as they could, trying to get everyone out and on the road.

By now my tongue was swollen and hurting. I could not close my mouth. My legs and feet were numb, except for pain deep inside them. My eyesight was blurred. It was hard to remember who I was or what I was doing. I still could not pick up my feet. In the background I could hear groans and cries but did not know why. It was as though I didn't have the strength to even look to see.

I just kept moving down a dirt road, one step at a time. Sometime later I could hear voices in front of me but was unable to tell what was happening. As I stumbled along knowing that my next step might be my last, someone took my arm. His voice was low, not a Japanese voice. My first thought was that both of us would be shot or bayoneted. Then it came to me that the voice belonged to Gerald. He said the march was over, that we were at Camp O'Donnell.

I lay on the ground. It was hard to see anything. Gerald put a wet cloth over my mouth and face, telling me that I was going to be all right. At every little noise my body would jump. I have no idea how long I was there on the ground. When I awoke, Gerald was putting a drink of water against my lips. My mouth was so dry and my tongue so swollen, when I took a swallow, it was like swallowing hot water. He only gave me some small sips for a while. Later he and another person moved me to a building and sat me up against it. Men were moaning and crying all around us. Gerald and I, along with some of the others, stayed by the building until the next morning. We then went inside a broken-down barracks that had grass mats on the floor.

— 5 —

Camp O'Donnell

A FEW DAYS PASSED. My tongue was getting back to normal, and I was getting a bowl of rice each day. There was only one water spigot in the camp for our water supply, and you had to line up for about an hour before you could reach it. If you sat down a Japanese guard would come over and make you get up. I was still very weak, but Gerald had helped me up to now with getting water and food.

Camp O'Donnell was a Filipino army post with shabbily built buildings. The one I was in had a bamboo floor about two feet off the ground. I understand that some buildings had dirt floors. As I got to the point where I could move around, I couldn't believe the condition of some of the men. Some were dying from the brutal death march, others were suffering from malaria, dengue fever, dysentery, malnutrition, scurvy, diphtheria, beriberi, ulcerated sores and blisters.

The bamboo floors were hard on our bodies. We had nothing to lay under us for padding. I had already lost about twenty pounds. When I went outside I could see that a hospital building had been set up. The men that went in found it was the last place for them, the end of the road, because they were going to die. Their clothes would be pulled off and the Japanese would slide their bodies under the building until they could be buried.

Soon the Japs were taking a few men on outside work details

if they were able to walk. A wire fence that had tall grass outside it surrounded the camp. Some Filipino soldiers did escape, but it was very risky if you were in bad shape and had no one on the outside to help you make it. If you tried to escape and were caught, you were shot. Some details would go out to work and when they returned, you would discover that the Japs had killed as many as five to ten of them that day. They were just left to rot by the side of the road, or maybe tossed into a ditch.

Many nights we would be awakened by the sounds of a Jap beating someone. They liked to use their rifle butts. Each lick resulted in the yells or moans that got weaker and weaker until you didn't hear them any more. The next morning someone had to get the body and put it under the hospital building until a burial detail could get to it. When the time came to do the burial, each body would be placed on an army blanket, then each end would be tied and a pole run through the knots. Two men would put the pole on their shoulders and take the body to a large shallow grave, lay it down by the side of the grave, slip the pole out, untie the blanket and roll the body into the grave on top of many others.

The whole area was covered with the sickly sweet smell of death. Dead human bodies have a very different odor from that of other dead creatures. Once you have been exposed to it, you will never forget it.

At times I would find a place to lie down in the sun, look up at the skies, and wonder if God was seeing what was happening here. I knew He had walked along with me on the march. Even though I was in bad shape, I didn't get shot or beaten like many of the other marchers. He gave me strength to resist the temptation of trying to get water, which would have resulted in being shot or bayoneted to death.

When I stopped to think, the feeling would go over me that I should just give up and go ahead and die. But it didn't happen that way. Every time my thoughts drifted in that direction, I would think of home and Jamie, and I would begin wondering if she came back from her visit, and whether or not she had gotten married. I would also think about what might have happened to Nelda, and if she was all right. Then I would think, I have to go and find out for myself. I must live and not let these Japs destroy me.

Each time a man would get close to death, he wanted to tell someone to talk to his family or loved ones and tell them how he had died. Soon we were burying over two hundred men a day in camp, plus the ones killed on the work details.

I was now able to work on the burial detail. I had two sets of dog tags, so knowing I might get killed outside the camp, I decided to throw a set into the mass grave there just in case. If my death did occur, at least my body would be identified as being in that grave, and would settle any questions from my family. I would not just be listed as missing in action with them not knowing whether or not I had made it. There would be no problem, and it would settle things for them.

As the days dragged on, the death rate climbed higher and higher. I knew I could not take it much longer, so Gerald and I decided to try to get outside by working on details and taking our chances. Some details left and never came back. That was the kind we wanted to get on and it didn't matter which one. We knew that in time if we stayed there in Camp O'Donnell, death would surely be our fate.

Some men from the 75th had also made the march. One of them was Howard Leachman, from Cartersville, Georgia. He had helped me so much during the fighting, since he was in charge of all the ammo going out of the warehouses. Some others from our company may have made it, too, but I was unable to go around looking for them.

Gerald and I won some pesos in card games, but there was very little you could buy. Some men that went out on daily work details would bring in things like canned goods. We paid as much as 250 pesos for one can of corned beef. We only bought one can at a time, because if you went to sleep, when you woke up your food would be gone.

I never dreamed that a person could stand such harsh treatment as we were given at the hand of the Japs, and still live. Every day at the water spigot there would be some men fighting over water and acting like animals. One would lose all sense of reality. Our bodies were wasting away. Sickness was rampant. Everyone knew that if something were not done soon, all of us would surely die. It was a fact that escape was out of the question because our bodies could not stand a run for freedom, so why try? Take what you were dealt if you could, or go try to take a rifle away from a Jap. If you were successful, you could shoot one or two of them, but after that, they would surely kill you.

Adjusting to this constant threat was impossible for most men, but if you gave up, you lived only a few days. You could look in most men's faces and see the horrors they had endured. There was a look of hopelessness on almost every face.

Soon they were calling for hundreds of men to go on details. These men didn't come back, so Gerald and I went out the next time and lined up. A guard came around shoving us into different groups, and Gerald and I were split up.   We had been together all the way through the fighting, stood side by side in battle, and saved each other's lives several times. Our friendship was the kind where you would step up to catch a bullet to save the other one. No one could say or do anything to the other without dealing with both of us.

Gerald was a strong and a brave man, yet he looked at me with tears in his eyes and I looked at him in the same way. I yelled at him and told him I would see him later. As we walked out the gate, he was standing there trying to get the guard to let him come with us, but had no luck. I found out months later that he went on a very bad detail at Nichols Field. I could not find out anything else.

The Japs loaded us onto trucks and we went to the railroad and got on flatcars, passed Manila, and went way south to southern Luzon. We were unloaded and made to march twenty or thirty miles into a dense jungle. It was nothing like The Death March, but we were weaker, and marching again took its toll on us. We were able to help each other, though, without being beaten or shot.

On the way we stopped at a schoolhouse. Three or four men were unable to go any further so they replaced them with six other Americans. We lost one man on the march. For all we know his body was left by the side of the road. There was no way for me to know where we were going or for what purpose. When we finally arrived at our destination, we found ourselves beside a river in the dense jungle somewhere in South Luzon. We were told we were there to build a road.

— 6 —

The Tayabas Road Detail

WHEN WE ARRIVED AT our new camp location, we found there were no buildings. The camp itself was located on the edge of a river, where the Japanese had a tent set up to use for their office and another one for their guards to bunk in. They also had horses at this camp.

We were taken to a bend in the river. There was an open space with rocks and sand, and we were told that we were to camp there. We thought we were to stay only for the night, but we found out it was our permanently assigned place to sleep. We were out in the open with only rocks and sand for our mattress. We had no materials to use to make a camp and were just to find a spot to lay our heads down as if we were animals instead of humans.

In addition, we were all told that guards would be there all night to watch us. We were placed in groups of ten men and warned that if any one or two were to try to escape, the rest would be shot. We made a pact that if anyone wanted to try to escape, all ten would go or none would try.

The next morning we were awakened at daybreak by the guards. The designated cooks were already cooking some watery rice. There was nothing large enough to cook in that would hold the food for all of us, so the cooks used a couple of steel wheelbarrows.

After we ate, we had to take these same wheelbarrows out and haul dirt and wood all day with them. To get drinking water we dug a small hole in the sand and let the water from the river fill it up by seeping into the hole. The problem was that the horses were located upstream from us and used the river to dispose of their waste, so that's what we had to drink. There was little iodine left to purify the water.

OUR ASSIGNMENT WAS TO build a road to connect southern Luzon with northern Luzon to make it possible for the Japanese to move troops by land rather than by water. We had picks, shovels, and jackhammers to drill the rock, and we had to break the large rocks with sledgehammers and pry bars.

They put us in work groups of about twenty, each with a guard. They had bosses that acted like engineers who went from group to group telling the men what to do. They picked out one American to be head of each group, but he had to work as well. If the boss came by, he would tell the one American what he wanted done by the group.

I was selected by the Japs to be the head of our group. We named the one Jap guard assigned to us Killer, because the second day, a man in another group could not lift the sledgehammer and hit a big rock hard enough to break the rock, so Killer knocked the American down. He fell on the rock. When he did, the Killer hit him in the back so hard that the rock crushed his chest in, and he was dead within thirty minutes. The guard would not let any of us help him. He just lay there on the rock and bled to death.

The guys continued to get sick. Conditions were so bad the doctor we had at the camp could not keep up with the problems. When the doctor would tell the Japanese that a man was too sick to go to work they would go to him and say, "No sick; work, or get beat." Some would drag out to work only to be beaten nearly to death. They would lie there until we brought them in with us when we quit work.

A couple of my close friends died at that camp. Howard Leachman called me to the spot where he was lying and asked me to do something for him. He said he was going to die and wanted me to go see his folks when I went home.

I tried to pep him up and tell him, "No, you are not going to die."

"Oh, yes, I am," he told me.

I knew that his health had not been very good before the Death March and had worsened since. "Everyone is saying this will be over in a few months," he told me, "but I see it differently. It's going to be a long siege for us."

I asked him why he had asked me to go see his folks, because he knew some men there better than he knew me. He said, "You are the only one here that I know will go home. Since you live in Alabama, you will also be the only one that if you promise to do this for me, it will be done. None of the others will fulfill my dying wishes, so please, promise me that you will."

So I told him, "Okay, I promise that I will."

He reached into his pocket and pulled out a beat-up billfold. He took out a picture of his son, who was born after he came to the Philippine Islands. He said, "This is my son. I've never seen him, but I love him. I want you to look him up when you get back and see if he is OK. If not, please promise me you will find my mother and father in Cartersville, Georgia, and see to it that they take care of him." There were problems between members of the family that concerned Howard and caused him to think that his son might not be well taken care of by his son's mother. He wanted his son to grow up in a Christian environment.

Each day when I came in from work, I would check on Howard. I kept trying to pep him up and assure him that he was not dying. Each time he would say he was dying and he knew he really was close to death. After a couple of days, one of the doctor's assistants came to me as I returned from work and told me I had better go see Leachman, that he was close to death.

When I got to Howard's side, he knew who I was, and said to me, "Now that you will take care of my wish, I can die knowing you will help my son. Please tell him I love him, and that I am sorry I couldn't tell him myself."

I told him again I would try to find his son and help him. As he smiled at me, he had tears running down his cheeks. I got together with three other men, and we said a prayer for him, asking God to take care of him and his son.

As I sat there beside him I could see the pain he was in. I also thought that his death might be for the best, as I could not see how anyone that sick could last long. His pulse became weaker and weaker, and soon it was over for another proud, brave soldier. I will never forget Leachman, nor will I forget his love for his son and how much he wanted to live to see him, and how much it meant to him that I would help his son when I got back to the States.

I WAS STILL ON the detail where Killer was beating men every day. Almost every day we had to carry at least three or four men with us who were unable to work. Soon my day came for the beating I had watched others get so many times. I think Killer had wanted to beat me for some time, but I had been very careful not to cross him. I knew what he was capable of doing.

We were on our way back to camp, marching four abreast. As we came to a narrow bridge across a deep ravine, Killer started yelling for us to go faster, even to run after we had worked all day. Our pace was bound to slow down from a four-column to two men side by side to walk across that narrow bridge. Since I was in charge of the Americans, I looked him in the face and said, "Shut up you blankety blank Jap!" He looked back at me and said something threatening in Japanese, which by now I understood.

He slapped me about four times, then along came a guard. He took his rifle butt and hit me in the chest hard enough to knock me down. The guard hit me three times, then Killer went over to a pile of tools and got a pry bar about five feet long and told the guard to step back. I was standing at attention when the bar hit me above my left eye as I tried to dodge the blow. I blacked out. The next thing I knew, I was in camp and the medic was putting a piece of tape across the cut, which was about three inches long. I could not see out of that eye.

I went in and out of consciousness for a couple of days. As soon as I could walk, they were trying to get me back to work. Then I decided on a way to get more time to get better before I had to go to work again. I would ask for help to stand up, then would fall and hobble around like I could not stand or walk. That act got me about six days' rest from having to go back to work. For some reason Killer didn't have much to do with me, for each time I was close to him, I would stare right into his eyes. I hope it frightened him.

My head was getting infected, and sometimes I could not keep my balance. When I would stumble walking to and from work the guards would push or slap me. When they hit my head the impact would open the cut over my eye and make it worse. It was months before it healed.

The big, black mosquitoes were another real problem. They were so bad that if you left any part of your body exposed at night they would cover that area completely. I saw men who looked like they had black masks over their faces, they were so covered with mosquitoes. It was hard to protect your entire body with just one blanket.

Out in the jungle there were patches of bananas. My place to sleep was at the back edge of the sleeping area. While I was in camp dealing with my head injury, I figured out a way to fix my bed so that it would look like I was asleep by piling up sand and rocks under the blanket in the shape of my body.

I would watch the guard when he made his rounds. The process of making rounds kept him away from my area for 45 minutes or an hour. I would slip out into the jungle and get a small bunch of bananas, bring them back close to my sleeping area and cover them up with leaves or some brush. When they were ripe enough to eat, I would slip out and bring in some, eat some of them, then cover up a few in the sand under my blanket for later. This helped control my dysentery.

ONE MORNING WE HEARD the Japs talking excitedly and found out that a Jap guard had been sitting under a tree the night before and that he had probably gone to sleep. Two pythons had wrapped themselves around him. By the next morning, one of the snakes had swallowed one leg and the other had his head in his mouth.

We told them that we had seen several big pythons in the jungle. After we made this statement, they posted a guard outside their shack at night. Several times we saw large pythons in the jungle area we were clearing during the day. The Japs would get excited every time one was spotted or they knew one was close by. Sometimes we would point and say one was out there. That would take a little pressure off us so we could slow down our work for a few minutes or so while they tried to find the python.

Out of 306 men in the Tayabas Road camp, about forty died the first month, but more and more men were becoming sick and were being beaten and starved. The American crew who worked in camp and who usually took care of the sick men were unable to take care of all of them. There were so many getting sick that most just lay there and got well all by themselves with no medicine or treatment, or else they died. When we buried someone, we just put two stakes like a cross at the head of the shallow graves and put the men's dog tags inside with them, figuring the graves would never be discovered by the Americans, even when the war was all over.

When the Japs wanted to speed us up at work, they would play a game with each other. Each Jap boss was supposed to get so much mud and rocks moved each day. If he got that amount done before quitting time, he got good marks from his commander, so he would promise us more rice or some rest if we worked faster and loaded our wheelbarrows quicker.

When all the wheelbarrows were loaded, the Japs would get out front yelling and running to beat the other bosses to the dumping area. This made it very hard on those of us who were unable to keep up. Some men would fall down and, being unable to run, they would be beaten. Some of the healthier prisoners who benefited from this system resisted changing it. In addition, the guys who ran the hospital area were withholding medicine from the sick men. They told the men that the Japs had refused them any medicine, but some of us saw the Japs give the medical men medicine that was never passed out to the sick. At times Americans would do harmful things to other Americans that would hurt them. Not only did we have to deal with the brutal Japs, but also the way some prisoners, frantic to survive, could turn against one another.

There were a couple of trucks that took some of the sick away. We found out later that these men had gone to Bilibid Prison in Manila.

All of us had bad cases of dysentery. We thought if we ate charcoal the dysentery would slow down. We had plenty of charcoal around, so we ate it every night, sitting around with black teeth and mouths. One guy was sitting there and started laughing. Someone asked what he was laughing about and he said, "I'll bet I've eaten a twleve-foot long 2 x 4, and all it is doing is making my crap blacker."

Some of the men were getting some help from the American medic, but getting any help for my injured head was difficult. All the medical personnel did for me was to put a piece of tape over a gash about three inches long. I think once they gave me some gauze and tape to make a new bandage.

There were reports of lots of food around, but for many of us, that was not the case. I can remember a few times when we got some corned beef, but it was so little that it didn't help much. It made the dysentery worse for some of the men. The situation soon reached the point where almost no one was able to work. The rainy season was coming, and there would be no work done during that time, so we were told we would be leaving shortly. That was good news to us.

There were about twenty-five men left at that point. One of them, Turesky, was almost dead. One day we were preparing to go, but the Japs kept us waiting. Turesky was a friend of mine. I went to the Japs and asked if we could load him on the truck. They told me no, that he was not going. I went to the doctor and asked about it. He said the Japs told him they were waiting for him to die, or had planned to shoot him. I begged them to let him go. At least he might have a chance to live. The waiting went on for a while and then the Japs grabbed me and slapped me several times. They took me back to the area where everyone was waiting. We found out later that the doctor talked them into letting him give Turesky a shot. I guess they left his body just lying there. We were helped into the trucks and taken to Bilibid Prison Camp in Manila.

All of us were ragged and in terrible shape. Our clothes were filthy, since they were never washed while we were there. Some clothes were wired together to keep them from falling off. I guess you could smell us quite a distance away. The Japs would not come close to us unless it was to hit us. None of us was able to get on the truck by ourselves. We tried to help each other, but still not all of us could get on, so the Japs brought two Filipinos to help us climb in.

The trip to Bilibid Prison in Manila was uneventful except that one guy died on the way. As we passed through small villages, the Filipinos would look and turn away. I saw some women put their hands over their noses and mouths and run back into the village. I guess we looked so bad they could not stand to look at us.

When we pulled into the gate at Bilibid, some American medics came out to see us. They turned and went back inside. We waited for a while because we were unable to get off the truck by ourselves. When they came back we were told that no one wanted to touch us because we were so nasty. They told us to get off the truck, sit on the ground, and wait. All the Japs who came out would look at us and turn around and go back inside.

Soon some Filipinos came out with a fire hose. We were told that they would try to wash off some of the filth before they could take us inside or give us any help. After our wash down, we were told to take off our clothes. So there we were sitting on the ground with only a blanket around us. Everyone came to look at us like we were some kind of freaks. I sure felt like one.

We were taken to an area of the building that was composed of one large room. The room had a concrete floor but nothing else in it. The concrete floor was where we were to sleep. By now I was down to about 145 pounds and my bones soon tried to come out through my skin. Big sores had developed all over my body.

Conditions, as bad as they were, were better at Bilibid Prison than they had been on the Tayabas Road detail. In addition, we heard a rumor that we would soon be getting some help, which was good news.

— 7 —

Bilibid Prison, Manila, P.I.

BY NOW I WAS IN very bad shape. Between the time of our stay at Camp O'Donnell and the Tayabas Road ordeal, we were unable to gain enough strength to do much physically. I realized that getting well was the most important thing I could do for myself if I expected to make it out of this place alive.

We had no belongings beyond the clothes on our backs and these were ragged and torn, and so dirty it was hard to tell if there was any color to them. Our bodies were dirty. We were not permitted to take a bath and most of the men were not able to bathe themselves anyway. Most of us had not been able to take a bath since our capture in Bataan. Our shoes were cracked open on the sides and the laces were gone. Most of us had to tie our shoes on with wire.

Most of the men had already had all the sicknesses usual to captured prisoners. Now my body began to swell, which meant I was starting to get beriberi, the wet type. The wet kind started in a person's feet. Soon his legs would start retaining water, and the swelling moved up the body. Then his lungs would start retaining water. When the water got to the victim's heart, he would die.

The dry beriberi would dehydrate bodily fluids. Well, I know my Guardian Angel was with me, for I got the wet beriberi on the bottom of my body and the dry kind on top. So I was dehydrated down to my waist. This condition was not common because you usually either had the wet or the dry, not both types. Your legs would swell to three or four times their normal size and you could push your thumb into your skin all the way to the bone. When you pulled your thumb out the hole would stay there for twenty or thirty minutes.

Most of the men who got beriberi had the wet kind. They knew if their diet was not changed soon, it was surely just a matter of time before death. All you could do was try to console them and try to give them hope.

At Bilibid Prison, we were divided up into groups, depending on how sick each of us was. I was put into a large room on the ground floor because I was too weak to walk up any stairs. My room had a concrete floor, and I was given nothing to use for padding under my body. I had lost about 40 pounds by now and weighed only about 135 pounds. As tall as I was, this weight meant my bones were showing. It was not long before I developed big spots all over my body and sores that were closest to where the bones touched the concrete floor.

I started having fever. The small ration of rice I received each day was not enough to help me get well nor was there any way to get food from some other place. However, at times we could get close to the outside wall, and we could hear people passing by. Some of us would start to tussle with each other to get the guard busy and divert his attention. We would get close to the wall and ask the Filipinos outside to throw over a few things to eat, like sugar cakes. If the guard from the tower saw them, he would yell or shout, but most of the time he didn't see us trying to get food. When they did see us doing this, a guard would come through our area searching for what had been thrown over the wall, but by that time we would have eaten it all up, and he would find nothing.

Anything and everything we could find or use helped us in the camp. Most men there had a "quan," which was like a one-gallon can. You could get some scrap food and fix up a brew using a quan. We would set three rocks down with a little space between them, build a small fire in the yard and cook up a brew. A guy gave me a quan just before he died, and I would fix him part of anything I could get and share it with him until his death. Sometimes we would get a few guys together to fix a brew. Whoever owned the quan can that was used to make the brew got a share of the prepared food, so owning a quan was very important.

We were always looking for something to eat. There were a few cats around, but soon they were in someone's quan pot making a little stew. Also, we heard that rats were being cooked. The few leaves on the trees were added for flavor.

When you see so many guys die, the first thing you start to wonder is when your turn will come. You try to figure which day will be the one when a Jap won't like the way you look or that you will do something to give him an excuse to beat you to death.

THE JAPS HAD A FEW Filipinos working around Bilibid. I was on the backside of our wardroom, and one of them came around to collect some trash. I asked him where he was from. He told me Alabang. That was close to where Nelda lived. I asked him to try to find her family and tell them where I was, and that I was still alive.

About two weeks later I saw the Filipino motioning for me to come around a building. He had to be very careful because if the guards saw him we would both be beaten or shot. He put a piece of paper under a rock. It took me about two hours to get back there and pick it up. When I finally was able to get to the place, I found a note from Nelda.

She said her family was involved in a guerilla battle against the

Japs. Her dad was one of the heads of a group operating close to Manila, and they would try to get some food smuggled into Bilibid. She also told me how much she loved me.

Her family had made it out of Bataan without much trouble except for the long walk they had to make. She and her friend tore their clothes and fixed their hair to look old so the Japs would not rape them. They also got help from other Filipinos along the way. Americans could do nothing to help them.

Having the note from her made me feel great, just thinking that someone cared about me. I sort of put my girlfriend back home out of my mind for that period of time, for now I was thinking, not *if* I would die, but *when*. All hope of making it back home had just about faded away. So what if I would have to stay in the Philippine Islands. Maybe getting back with Nelda would be a good thing. But at times thoughts of going home would bug me. Maybe hope of any kind was the only thing that kept me alive.

Word came to me later from a Sergeant in Bilibid Prison after I was already in Japan, that Nelda's family raided the prison looking for me. He said all of them got away, but supposedly a couple of Jap guards were killed.

Bilibid Prison was a terrible place. A doctor there told us it was twenty times worse than during the time before the war when they had animals there, and at that time it had some of the worst health conditions in the world. You know it was bad. I got to where I could sleep on the concrete floor, but my body sores wouldn't get better. I guess I kept my weight about the same, and slowly my beriberi did improve a little.

I got word that Nelda's brother was going to throw some oranges over the wall one at a time and for me to watch for them at a certain day and time. We set the time for noon because the guards were making some changes then, and I would know when 12 o'clock noon would come by the bells from a church nearby that would ring. We used all the things around us to our advantage. I still do not know how Nelda's brother could get the things over the wall because it was high, but it sure was a lifesaver and, to some extent, helped me get my sickness under control.

At times I would wonder what it would be like to get out and return home, have a good meal, see my family, and ask my girlfriend for forgiveness for leaving—in case she had come back from her trip still not engaged. Or if she had gotten married, I wanted to wish her good luck.

There was a guy at Bilibid whom I remembered from the front lines with the Philippine Army when we set up an ammunition dump sometime in January, 1942. He was full of life and a great soldier who had fought with all his might against the advancing Japanese forces. It was so sad to see this brave man now lying there wasting away with sickness. He asked me many times to pray for him; he said that he was a big sinner, and he thought he needed to have someone else ask God to forgive him.

I kept telling him to ask God for forgiveness himself, and I know he did. When I showed up on the list to go to Japan, he begged me not to leave him. The day we were to leave I went to see him, only to find that he had died. I thought back to the number of times he would say how much he wanted to go home. How humble a man gets when he thinks he is about to die.

IT WAS SOMETIME IN October, 1942. I had time at Bilibid to think about all that had happened to me. My thoughts would go back to the Death March, the men whom I had liked that had gotten killed or some of the men that I lost contact with. My body was in terrible shape, and my mind would drift. Sometimes it was hard to remember my own brothers' and sisters' names.

I would think about how God had taken care of me so far. I thought, too, about some of the Americans who were on the Tayabas Road detail who had withheld medicine from the sick, and who died themselves there in Bilibid. They had seemed to be in good shape when we came back from Tayabas, but it made me think that God had His way of handling the ones who ignored His rules. It was as though He pointed His finger at them and justice was done.

As we lined up to move out to go to Japan, there were fifty of us in the group. We were loaded onto a truck and were taken to the Manila docks and loaded onto a small freighter. As we walked up the gangplank I thought about how I felt. My spirit was broken, my health was very bad, and I was going into God knows what, into a land that I knew would be the last place Americans would come if and when this terrible war came to an end.

How can a man stand tall with self-pride when he has been stripped of his dignity, broken by being starved, worked in slave labor camps, defeated in battle, and disgraced by his captors? Now I would be going to a land that had no friendly faces such as the Filipinos had when we were able to see them.

Just before we left, a captain said to me, "When you get there, you tell them you were a cook. Never tell anything else, Corporal. Tell them you were a cook because if they find out you killed a Jap or had anything to do with killing any on Bataan, they will shoot you on the spot."

As we boarded the small freighter we were put down in a freight hole on top of lumber and other things they were taking to Japan. A latrine was put on the side of the ship's deck for our bathroom. With us was a wonderful navy commander by the name of Callahan.

I didn't know him in Bilibid, but it didn't take but a short time to get to like him.

We also had an army captain and a first lieutenant with us. The Japanese guards were not as bad as the ones we had before, so they would let us up on deck at times. Our ration was a small amount of rice just once a day. With this meager ration we could not gain much strength, but just holding our own was good enough, and we thanked God for that.

There were seven ships in our convoy, along with a small gunship. Our ship had only one three-foot gun on the front deck. Commander Callahan found out that the gun would only turn 45 degrees to each side. He was also the Communication Officer for the Far East and knew that submarines would be in the waters. He got us all together down in the hold and asked what each of us did during the war and what training we had. We had a radio operator with us, and a few navy guys that had been trained as gunners on American ships.

Commander Callahan had a plan to watch the gunboat and when it got in the right position, the three-foot gun on deck would turn just enough so that we could fire at the gunboat. We planned to take over the radio room and overpower the guards and crew. His idea was to get on the radio and contact any American subs, and try to get one of them to pick us up. On our cleanup details we were able to find out what kind of radio was aboard and where the ammunition for the guns was stored.

We would ask the one guard at night on top of the hold to let someone go to the latrine so they could look to see where the gunboat was. Commander Callahan would stay up at night trying to get the guard to let him go on deck. Because he was the ranking officer, they sometimes permitted this. When we got close to Formosa we had a submarine alert, but no shots were fired. We never did get the gunboat into a position where we could execute our plan.

I'm not sure exactly when in October we left Manila, but I do remember it was the 2nd of November, 1942, when we arrived at Moje, Japan, where we were loaded onto a train. It was cold and we had no warm clothes. Our rail car was like a livestock car with openings in the sides so that the cold air coming in almost froze us to death. While we were in the railroad depot, the Japs would yell at us. Small kids would spit at us as we passed them.

When we arrived at our destination we saw a sign on a building saying that this was Osaka, Japan. We were taken to Osaka #1 POW Camp. As we lined up in front of the main building there were many guards, as well as other persons who were wearing regular clothing. One very ugly person was going around acting like he was the organizer. We would say things like look at that ugly Jap, and make statements like, "At least we had some nice-looking guards in the Philippine Islands."

Soon a Jap colonel came out with about three other people. They put a two-foot stool out in front of us. The colonel stepped up on the stool. The ugly one stood beside him and said in English, "Let's have your attention; I'm your interpreter."

The old Jap colonel started his talk about how wonderfully we would be treated here. We were considered to be guests of the Emperor of Japan, and if we did not obey his and all the guards' orders, we would be punished. If we attempted to escape the escapee and nine others in our group would be shot.

Mr. Ugly talked as though he was from America, using perfect English. The talk went on for about thirty minutes. It was the same old bull we were told when we had first arrived at Camp O'Donnell. Bilibid was a staging area for persons going to Japan.

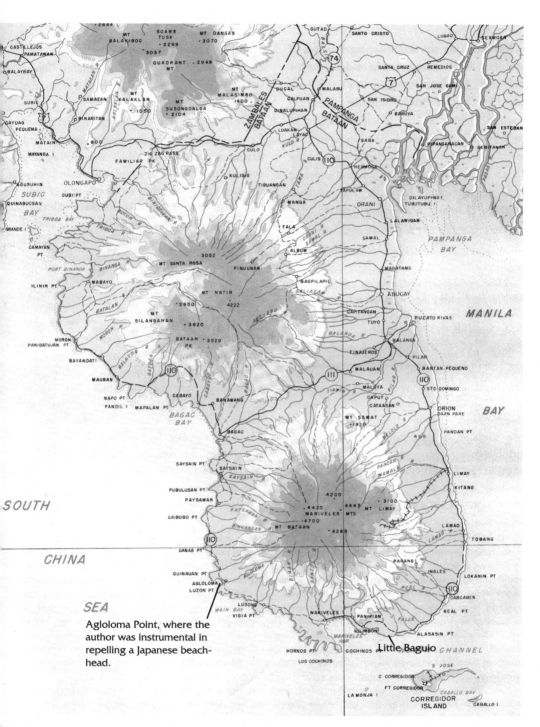

Agloloma Point, where the author was instrumental in repelling a Japanese beach-head.

The Bataan peninsula, site of the heroic resistance of American forces against the overwhelming numbers of the Japanese. Shown are the locations of Agloloma Point and Little Baguio, site of American field headquarters on Bataan.

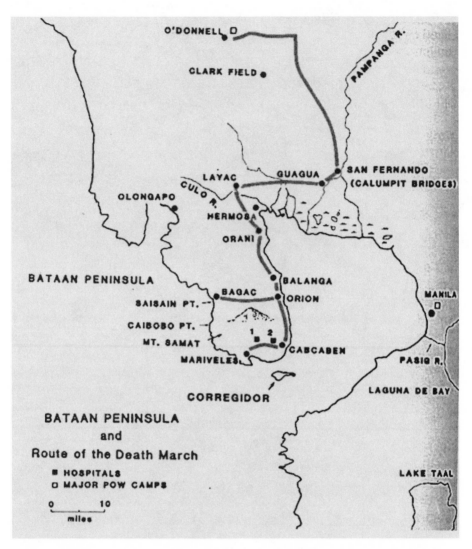

O'DONNELL □

CLARK FIELD ●

PAMPANGA R.

GUAGUA

LAYAC

CULO R.

OLONGAPO

HERMOSA

ORANI

SAN FERNANDO
(CALUMPIT BRIDGES)

BATAAN PENINSULA

SAISAIN PT. →

CAIBOBO PT. →

MT. SAMAT

BAGAC

BALANGA

ORION

1 2
■ ■

MANILA
□

CABCABEN

MARIVELES

CORREGIDOR

PASIG R.

LAGUNA DE BAY

BATAAN PENINSULA
and
Route of the Death March

■ HOSPITALS
□ MAJOR POW CAMPS

0   10
miles

LAKE TAAL

The route of the Death March. It started at Miraveles on the southern tip of Bataan and went north and west to San Fernando. At San Fernando the prisoners were loaded onto boxcars and taken to Camp O'Donnell.

Frazier played tackle on the Fort Deposit High School football team.
His size (over six feet tall) and his physical strength probably saved
his life many times over during his years as a POW.

Left: A Japanese photographer snapped this photograph during the Death March. Circled are Glenn Frazier (in front) and Gerald Block (with the towel around his neck).

Below: Prisoners sit for a rare rest along the route of the Death March. Their hands appear to be tied behind them.

Left: A burial detail at Camp O'Donnell. Bodies of dead POWs were put under the hospital building, then collected and taken to be buried. There is a body in each of the blankets.

Below: Beheadings such as this one were not uncommon. Glenn Frazier narrowly escaped this kind of death.

Left: This drawing accurately depicts the kind of beating suffered by POWs at the whim of their guards. Only the strongest survived.

Below: Two POWs hours after their liberation. These men were the healthy ones.

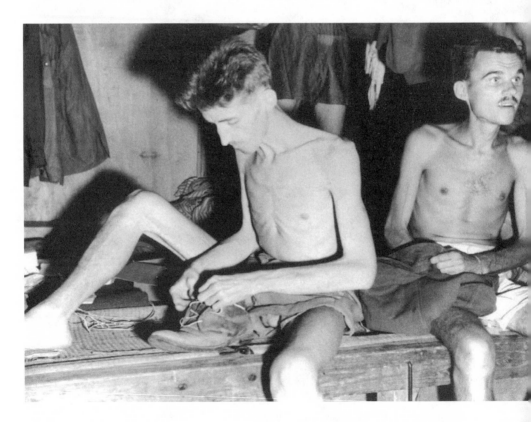

Sgt. Glenn Frazier after his homecoming. By this time he had regained the weight he lost in the prison camps.

Glenn Frazier in 2003. He is wearing the uniform of a colonel in the Alabama Defense Force and the Medal of Freedom awarded by the United States Senate.

— 8 —

Osaka #1 Camp

WHEN WE FIRST SAW Osaka #1, our hopes rose. It looked as though there was a building we might get to sleep in, and that there might be something to sleep on besides sand and rocks or a concrete floor. As the camp commander brought his speech to an end, he told us that we should consider ourselves "guests of their empire." Though we should have known better by this time than to believe anything we were told in a prison camp, his words made us feel better. Our interpreter—who had attended the University of Southern California and could speak English—told us to form into small groups and warned us he would not tolerate anyone who did not follow orders.

Commander Callahan stepped forward and gave the Japanese colonel a salute. The colonel told the interpreter to tell Commander Callahan to bow. Commander Callahan told him that the Geneva Convention said a captured officer was to salute his captor and did not say he had to bow. So our commander was taken to the office.

We stood in the parade ground for twenty minutes or so then were taken into the building by a guard. This would be our sleeping quarters. It had dirt floors and a long table down the center. On each side were sleeping bays, four bays high on each side of the table with ladders for climbing up into your bunk. The bunks were wood-floored with straw mats. There was in reality very little padding, but at first seemed to be better than anything we had had before. We had just enough space to lie down and room to turn over. Our shoes had to stay on the dirt floor at the foot of our bay.

The latrine and bath area consisted of a long slit trench and two spigots to take a shower with cold water. A chance to bathe was better than any arrangements we had before now. Most of us were thinking this sure was an improvement over what we had survived in the Philippines, but the guards' talk was tough and a guard was yelling at us about each little matter, pushing and shoving us around with his rifle butt.

Soon the hope came over me that maybe here I would have a chance to get better. Also, my hopes were that maybe I would get to go back to the States after all. I was wondering how Nelda was doing and also what they had done when they found out I was no longer at Bilibid Prison. I was afraid they might have thought I had died.

I had to dismiss all these thoughts from my mind. After all, I was still in poor health and the most important thing at hand was staying alive. There and then, I made up my mind that they were not going to bury me on Japanese soil.

The first few days we got a good-sized bowl of rice in the morning and also a rice ball and a bread bun for lunch. Then at night we got a little more rice than was in our breakfast bowl. We were up at 5:30. We got dressed and were taken to the parade ground for our morning exercise. Our old clothes were taken away and we were given a Japanese soldier's uniform, used of course and already filled with body lice eggs. It didn't take long to let you know you were never alone with them crawling up and down your body day and night.

It was cold in Japan then and our clothes were not adequate to keep us warm. Our barracks did not have heat. We had to bundle up together at night with our clothes on to stay halfway warm. The guards would come in our barracks a few times at night and make us get back to our own bays. As soon as they would leave we would pile up again.

After Camp O'Donnell and the Tayabas Road detail I had no close friends left with me, but it didn't take long to find new good friends. It was easier to find someone you could trust when we had all been prisoners of war as long as we had. We were given a POW number. Mine was #632. Our pictures were taken and we were divided into groups of ten. We had to buck up and just try to make it day by day.

Gradually our familiarity with words that were used regularly by the Japanese soldiers made it easier to understand them. "Old Ugly" understood every word we would say. At first we thought maybe he would be good for us, but he turned out to be the opposite. He would get the guards to beat us for any little thing. When Old Ugly would turn to walk away someone would say, "Just wait until the USA wins this war, then we will kick your butt." He would turn around fast and try to find out who had spoken, but no one would tell him. There was no one in the camp who did not hate him.

They gave us four civilian guards. They were not soldiers but had a uniform that looked military, and they had as much power with the old Jap colonel as anyone else in the camp.

Our work details went out each morning about 6:30, and came in about dark. Our work in Osaka was unloading ships, loading and unloading railroad cars, and working in lumberyards, foundries and factories. Anything that came up, they had us doing it. It was hard work, and sometimes the bosses where we were working took the liberty to stand us up and beat a couple of the men for some little thing. I think they just wanted to beat an American. The guards would stand by and did nothing to stop them.

Our way of getting even was to destroy anything we could

"accidentally on purpose." On one occasion a Jap was up on a ladder in a foundry trying to fix an electric crane. A POW ran by the switch close to the door and turned it on. The charge knocked the electrician off the ladder and sent him to the hospital.

After a week at Osaka they stopped serving us our noon bun. We were told we would get more rice, but they didn't give us more. Commander Callahan told us we were not going to work; he said we would go on strike to get our buns back. He told us he would report to the camp commander's office and simply tell him "no buns, no work." He told us not to move or go anywhere until he told us to. If we disobeyed his order, he would deal with us as hard as the Japs would.

We just knew he would be beaten badly and that all of us would get the same. But soon he came back and said our rice would be increased at each meal. We won. But little did we know that our rice from then on would have worms in it. At first we covered up the little white worms with their black eyes looking at us, but soon we would just eat them as though they were added meat.

As the winter wore into February, 1942, it got bitterly cold. The north wind would blow right through our Japanese clothes. Most of us put cement bag paper inside our clothes next to our body to help stop the cold air, and it helped a great deal. Some of us got sick. In fact, I had double pneumonia and could not go to work. I lay in what was the sickbay area for three weeks with a high fever, sweating and then getting cold. I was so sick I didn't realize how bad off I was. Commander Callahan did get me some oranges but could not get anything that would break the fever. It's a wonder I made it. Perhaps the fact that I was so young was in my favor. When I went back to work I was so weak, I was limited as to how much I could do, so I was beaten just about every day for a week or so. Sick or hungry, I was ordered to work and withstand the constant beatings. The Japanese soldiers used their rifle butts to hit us whenever they felt like it. They would also dip their bare hands into cold water and slap our tired faces at an angle that made our faces swell abruptly.

ONE DAY I WAS marching with other prisoners through the streets of Osaka, returning from that day's work. It was bitterly cold and my hands became numb. I placed my lifeless hands into the pockets of my ragged pants. As I entered the camp gates, I noticed a Japanese guard pointing his finger at me, calling me to the attention of another guard. Later, in formation along with the other American POWs, I noticed the same guard pointing at me and walking in my direction. He instructed me to follow him. I really didn't think much about this at first. I followed the guard into the camp commander's office with the interpreter walking beside me. I was ordered to come to attention and bow to the major, who was sitting at his desk. A few moments later, the interpreter came over to me and said, "You were marching down the road with your hands in your pockets, and that is not permitted for Japanese soldiers."

I replied, "I'm not a Japanese soldier. I'm a prisoner of war!"

After hearing the major shout in Japanese to the interpreter, I was told in English by the interpreter, "The same rules apply to all POWs!"

"I didn't know that," I answered. In a faint voice I told the interpreter, "Why don't they tell us their rules?" To myself I thought, if I knew all the rules I wouldn't break them.

The major screamed at the interpreter, who translated: "You are an American soldier and you do not march with hands in pockets!"

I responded bluntly, "Let me know the regulations, and I will obey."

The interpreter translated my answer for the major. With a shocked look on his face the major jumped out of his chair and whacked his clenched fist on top of the desk. I knew now that I had really provoked him. By the manner in which he spoke to the translator, I could tell he wasn't thrilled by my attitude. He arose again quickly from his seat and walked toward me, and the guard made me bow once more.

The interpreter said, "The commander does not like your attitude!" At that point, the major pulled his sword out and nicked my throat. I felt the blood streaming down my neck.

"Prisoners can be executed for disobeying orders!" the interpreter continued. All I could do was stand still with thoughts of terror running through my mind. I stared into the major's hateful eyes. I never took my eyes off him, not for a moment.

All of this, for just walking with my hands in my pockets. A strange feeling came over me, and I suddenly knew this was a very serious matter. The major yelled at the guard, "Take him outside. I do not want blood all over my floor!" I began walking out of the office, with the rifle point of the guard behind me pressing into my back. He then ordered me to stop. I came to a complete halt, as instructed. I stood there waiting at attention for the next command, when I began thinking of and seeing myself buried in Japanese soil. My mind raced and I felt an immense fear, but somehow I felt I had a fighting chance.

I heard the commander and interpreter coming out adjacent to where I was standing. As they were speaking back and forth in Japanese, all I could do was stand still. I was then ordered by the guard to bow one more time to the major.

"The major is going to execute you, so all of the men will know that breaking regulations won't be tolerated!" the interpreter announced. The major walked in front of me and pulled his sword out again

122

and put it to my throat. They expected me to beg for mercy. The interpreter asked, "Do you have anything to say?"

"I guess," I told the interpreter, as I looked into the major's eyes. And then these words came to me, and to this day I have no idea where the came from. *"He can kill me," I replied, "but he will not kill my spirit, and my spirit will lodge inside him and haunt him for the rest of his life!"*

I was asked by the translator to repeat what I had uttered. A terrifying feeling came over me instantly, and my blood flushed over my entire body, making me absolutely burn with horror.

I said, still staring into the major's eyes, *"He can kill me but he will not kill my spirit and my spirit will lodge in his flesh for his entire life! The Americans are coming and any Japanese who kills an American without just cause will have their spirit haunt them forever!"*

I did not grasp at first what I had actually said. I was prepared to dodge the sword if the major made a move to swing it at me. I watched his every move, never taking my eyes off of him. All of a sudden, a mysterious expression appeared on the major's face. Then, to my amazement, the major made three steps back and lowered his sword. I gazed up to the sky and said, "Thank you, Lord." This was the first time I had seen a Japanese soldier back off from an execution.

The major then ordered the guard to take me to the pit in the earth that was used for solitary confinement. The guard, with his weapon shoved into my back, thrust me towards the 5' x 5' x 5' hole in the ground. As the Japanese guard lifted the cover to the hole, I wasn't sure that this ordeal was finished. He motioned for me to get down inside. Looking down into the depths of that dark place, I tried to get in. I landed head first, face down, after being pushed or kicked by the guard. My face and neck were hurting badly as I wiped the tears from my eyes.

I had been given no food or water since early that morning. The cover to the hole was shut and bolted down. It became pitch black. My body started shaking all over as I tried to get comfortable in such a cramped place. Soon the truth of what had just happened settled in my bewildered and hopeless mind. Everything had happened so fast, but I was grateful I was still alive. However, I waited with the fear that they would come back to finish the job the next day.

I lay there in darkness for seven days in my own body waste, hot, exhausted and frail. A small scrap of rice ball was thrown into the hole from time to time, and I had to squint my eyes from the light of the sun when the cover was unlocked and raised. I remember having a half-filled bottle of water thrown down that was close to me at all times. I sipped it cautiously. It was difficult to keep track of time. What day was it? I didn't know. Each time I heard a sound, I wondered what was coming. When will this trial end? I wondered. How drawn out will this suffering be? Dying seemed effortless compared to the torment that was inflicted on me.

Being isolated in the darkness of the hole, my memory played tricks on me. At times I thought of home and my family back in Alabama. They seemed so far away, I couldn't remember my brothers' and sisters' names. Did I actually have a family with brothers and sisters, I wondered. Most of the time I felt myself in a strange world, far removed from the place I remembered that I called home.

Without warning, the cover was opened and I thought, "What now? Is this the end?" And from the depth of my soul, I prayed it was. As the bright sunlight filled the entire hole, I saw the outline of someone who turned out to be a guard. His silhouette looked dim. Dehydration was making my body feel numb, and it seemed too strenuous to stand on my feet. Each time I tried, I felt feeble, dizzy and nauseated. I finally was able to get one hand placed on top of the outside of the rim of the hole. The Jap guard stomped on my hand and screamed at me, "Get out!" My legs wouldn't stop shaking. It was so hard to stand on my feet. As I placed my second hand on the rim of the dirt hole, he yanked both of my hands and dragged my lifeless and weakened body out on the ground. He kept kicking my side with his booted foot as I lay there semi-conscious. I felt my body roll over with my back on the dirt after he kicked me so hard. Still shouting at me, he gave me a lick on the head with his rifle butt, and I fainted.

I have no idea how long I lay there unconscious. I could see the barracks in the background when my vision started returning, but I didn't have the energy to rise to my feet. As I started to crawl on my hands and knees, I heard footsteps coming from behind me. The continuous screams from the guard with his forceful rifle butt knocking at my hips, legs and back, were so powerful my body moved with each blow. I was merely making an effort to reach the barracks where I knew one of my fellow POWs could help me.

Again my sight grew dim. After the grueling pain, I gained enough strength to crawl once more. I had gotten to the point where I could have begged the guard to shoot me. I had no way of telling how long it took me to finally get close to the barracks, but I finally felt someone pulling me along. I hoped it was one of the POWs. Sure enough, I had made it to the barracks where I was given a drink of water. What an awesome feeling to have someone do such a simple thing as give me a drink of water when I was one breath away from death.

As I lay for days in the area we called the sick bay, my mind and thoughts were that I must get back to work. I realized how close to death I was, and if I wanted to come back to the USA, I must control what I said and did. I decided not to get mad ever again. I would just get even.

There were many things that made it hard to control ourselves.

As we would walk down the streets, the little kids would run out shouting and cursing us, kicking us and spitting on us. They had been told that we were American cowards, dishonored by our country and that we were unable ever to go back to America.

As time went on, life was not much better there at Osaka. Our lives were threatened every day and night. The guards would change every two weeks, and the new ones might have been on the front lines and were very bitter about Americans, so this duty was their chance to get even with us.

One of the ways the guards punished us was by getting a large piece of railroad iron and making us stand at attention while holding the piece of iron over our heads as long as possible. When we could no longer hold it up and dropped the iron, they would give us a good beating.

By now we had learned some things that would help us, like growing a beard to protect our faces. We also discovered that when you were going to get a beating, you should always look the Jap straight in the eyes. Never look to one side or the other. If you did they would try to knock your head off.

Several Americans also tried to make friends with the Japs and report things to them that caused the Japs to beat several other men nearly to death. So we formed a group to take care of those Americans when they did this.

Since we received so little food, we became real thieves. We would steal any food we could find in the factories where we worked or from a carelessly placed Jap lunch box. To get a good plate of rice and fish was worth a good beating.

Almost every man had a six-inch hollow bamboo cane with a point on one end. While unloading ships or railroad cars that had rice in bags made of straw, we would back up to a stack of rice sacks as though we were resting for a few minutes or so. We called these bamboo sticks our bird callers. The pointed end would go between the straws in the straw sack into where the rice was. We would just bump the sack with our elbow and the rice or beans would flow into our pockets. If the Japs came toward us all we had to do was pull our bird caller out of the rice sack and hit the bag with our elbow and the sack would close as though it had not been touched. Then we would eat the raw beans or rice. When on this type of detail, we could manage a mouthful at times. We all became the best thieves in Japan. We could steal while they looked at us.

We always needed more food and when we went on details where there was nothing you could steal to eat, we put another plan into action. We would rotate the "fainting trick." Someone would faint each day, and the rest of us would have to carry the "sick" man back to the camp on a litter.

Well, we had a big coward in our group who didn't have the guts to faint because it would mean a beating by the guards on the detail or when we got back to camp, whether they could prove we fainted on purpose or not. So when the day came for our group coward and he would not faint, a guy from Chicago who weighed about 180 pounds, took it upon himself to fill in for him. Soon we heard a big commotion out behind a large stack of lumber. There was our 180-pound friend laid out faking a faint. Not only did he make it pretty clear that all our fainting was fake, as relatively healthy as he was, but we were all lined up and given a good slapping and kicking, after which we had to lug that big guy several miles back to our quarters on a stretcher. With his weight, it was not an easy job.

THE WINTERS GOT SO cold that it was not possible to take a bath or ever get completely warm. With all of us stacked up like a pile of pigs in camp, we still were cold. The bad thing about piling up to sleep was that someone had to go to the latrine every five minutes, so our sleep was limited at its best. Under these conditions, nearly all of us were sick to some degree, and a few were always very dangerously ill. We had no one to rely on but ourselves, so we came up with various ways to help the sickest ones get better.

One of the best techniques we came up with was a kind of laying on of hands that I called acupressure. I don't remember who first had the idea but it may have been a guy from Minnesota who was a Blackfoot Indian. When someone desperately needed help, one of us would cup his hand and place it over the navel of the man we were trying to help. We would hold our hand there for about thirty minutes. After a while our hand would grow hotter and hotter and the belly of the sick man would, too. We often found this technique to be amazingly effective, and sometimes the prisoner who had been sick would be up and around the next day. This was easy for us to do, since we slept so close together that it was easy to reach over and help the man next to you.

THERE WERE TIMES THAT a detail had to go a longer distance to work. They had a Jap driver we called Barney Oldfield, after the old race car driver. He drove that old charcoal burner truck as fast as it would go. The brakes were not so good and many times he had to drive off the road to keep from hitting a car or bicycle or buggy. Well, one day he showed up with a stake-body truck that used gasoline. There was room for about twenty-five of us POWs. The road to our work detail took us down a long, straight road alongside a train loaded with Japanese people. They started to yell at Barney. The train engineer blew his whistle. Barney blew his horn. The race was on. Here we were in the back, yelling for him to slow down, but he was enjoying the race.

The more our speed picked up, the more excited the people on the train became. What we did not know was that our road had to cross the railroad tracks ahead, and at the speed we were going, there was going to be a great collision soon if the train didn't slow down or if Barney didn't slow down. Some of us were standing up yelling for him to cross the tracks ahead of the train. There was no way at the speed we were going to get safely out of the truck.

As we approached the crossing, the train was blowing its whistle. Barney crossed the tracks as the train hit the right, rear corner of the stake body on the truck. It slung the right side of the truck body into the ditch. The train kept going. Barney pulled over for all of us to get off the truck—at which time we all had to go excuse ourselves! Lucky enough, only one of us got hurt, and that was because he fell off the truck.

IN OUR CAMP THERE were about thirty-five East Indians. We referred to them as Hindus. They were seamen on British ships that were sunk and who had been fished out of the water and brought to Japan. These Indians had the right idea. They could speak English but would never speak it in front of a Jap interpreter. So when the Japs wanted to work them, it was a circus. The Japs could not make the Indians understand any orders because they did not want to. Even a Jap who could speak English could not get them to understand.

Sometimes they would be across the fence from us on a detail and the Japs would start to beat one of them and the entire group would get in the middle talking that Hindi language, and it was like a free-for-all fight. The Japs did not treat them like they treated the Americans. If it had been us they would have started shooting. But with the Hindus they would have a time trying to get them to work. It would take two or three Hindus to carry one ten foot long two by four. The Japs would yell "Hi yaka," which meant "hurry." At this, the Hindus would stop, put down the two x fours, and send one man over to the Jap asking what "Hi yaka" was all about!

One day the truck the Hindus were riding in was hit by another truck. All of them were hurt some. When they arrived in camp you never heard such a racket as them complaining in Hindi. No one could understand all of them talking at one time!

Every morning in the cold of winter they would get up, go to the shower spigots and take a bath in that cold, cold water. They explained that they were washing away all the evil spirits for the day. We were so cold we could not take a shower at any time, but somehow these Hindus could manage it.

Osaka #1 was also used to house merchant seamen whose ships had been sunk by German raiders on the high seas. The sailors who survived the sinking were fished from the water by the Germans and somehow found their way to Osaka #1. They told stories of the Germans machine-gunning many of them in the water before others were picked up. We had just about every nationality at Osaka, and they all had their stories to tell.

BY NOW WE WERE also getting to know which Americans you could trust. We got together in groups of people who wanted to do things to the Japs for the way they treated us. We developed a plan that probably had no chance of succeeding, but one we were hoping we could get away with. What we wanted was to have accidents on purpose that would look like regular accidents. In our plan it was understood that none of us would try to do a job that a Japanese was doing because then they could send the Jap off to the Army.

We would try to disrupt the war effort in any way we could and destroy anything that would have to be replaced to keep production going. We would steal anything of value or break it beyond repair.

An example: once we were unloading machines from freight cars. The Japs told us that the equipment had come from Britain and that parts were not available to them, so the handles must be protected. That was a good project for us. We planned to get to this machinery before it left the yard and break every handle on every one of them. To hide the damage we loaded the equipment with the fronts to the truck's side body so the Japs could not see if the handles were broken or not. Before the trucks left the yard every handle was broken or thrown away.

If they left a truck unattended with the hood up we would do our best to fill the oil supply with as much sand as we had time to pour in it. Many times they would unload wooden barrels of liquid. It did not matter to us what was in these barrels. If it was about quitting time, we would make some kind of hole in the bottom of a barrel. By the next morning the liquid would be gone. Sometimes the liquid would not soak into the ground and a boss might question some of us about the incident. We had all kinds of answers for the guards. If a Jap or Korean worked the day before but was not there when the damage was found, we tried to put the blame on him. Sometimes we would get beaten anyway.

To do some of the things we did, sometimes we had to start a fight among ourselves to draw their attention away from where we were doing damage to something. We had to distract them anyway we could.

One day the guards pulled us out into the parade ground for what they called "drills." Old Ugly the translator told us we were never going back to America and that we needed to start learning more Japanese and how to march and obey drill orders. What a total flop that was. We were about like the Hindus, so the last thing they wanted us to do was the goose step—lifting your knees high against our chests then slamming our feet down against the ground. They also wanted us to speed up our steps. None of us were in any shape to do that.

Before I thought about what I was doing I slid my feet without picking them up at all. A Jap with his fixed bayonet came running toward me and stuck his bayonet into my knee, cut a gash about two inches long, and the tip of the blade went all the way to the bone. I was unable to move my leg. As I rolled on the ground I felt his boot hitting me in the back. Within a minute I was unable to get to my feet. The guard made me lie there until the drill was over, then had two other POWs drag me to the barracks by my arms.

Commander Callahan came out demanding that they let the POWs bring me to the sick bay area. It took about four weeks before I could walk on that leg. That's when I realized that without working, I would slowly drift into being unable to get around. The next step after that would be death. So hip-hopping or not, I had to get out of there. The wound turned blue, but I didn't tell the American doctor until later.

The British had a camp back of our Camp #1. Our fence was the only thing separating us from them. They were there long before we Americans arrived. We did not know for a while that they were getting our rice and cooking it. We did know that they looked in pretty good shape. So we kept looking through the fence to see what type and how much rice they were getting each meal. We found out they were getting twice as much as we were.

We talked this situation over with our Commander Callahan. He took it up with the old Jap colonel, only to be told that we were already getting enough rice. So we talked Old Ugly into getting us permission to visit our British friends.

Now there were about 350 of them and only 75 Americans in our camp, not counting the Hindus and other nationalities there. When we got a day that we did not have to work, they let us go over to see our "friends." As the gates opened we rushed in with blood in our eyes. Instead of passing out handshakes, we started a big fight.

As we fanned out, they started running, begging us not to fight them. Soon the Sgt. Major came forward asking why we wanted to fight his men. We told him about the ration we were getting and demanded our fair share. Before the guards could get us out we had kicked or hit just about everyone there. The Sgt. Major agreed he would fix the ration problem, and sure enough we got more rice.

As WE WOULD GO to work, we would often see a Jap soldier walking down the street with an American Red Cross box under his arm. At that time we had never received anything from the Red Cross. This made me feel like another mistake had been made by our country, sending boxes for us, but permitting the Japs to eat them and not give us anything.

Later, I received one box from home. What a wonderful thrill. It had a picture of my mother, dad, sister and a couple cousins. A letter was inside that was marked all over by the Japs, but was still from home. This brought back so many memories. My body system was so low that when I ate one chocolate Hershey bar it made my face flush. My body felt like I was on fire. What a reaction to a five-cent candy bar.

When I was eleven years old my leg was cut with an axe at school, and I had to stay in bed for two weeks. During my time at home, my mother showed me how to crochet a rug. Well, I had an old pair of wool pants, so I cut them up and made a crude-looking helmet with earflaps coming down over my ears. Some of the guys wanted me to give it to them if I died. As we walked through the streets of Osaka, the people would laugh at my helmet, but it sure kept my head warm. It was the only part of my body that was warm.

Osaka was where I learned the koolie trot. When they made you use the Yaho pole to carry something, you needed to do the koolie trot if it were a liquid you were carrying. A Yaho pole is a stick about six-feet long that you put over your shoulders. It has a rope at each end about two or three feet long with a bucket. You could hold one rope in front of you with your right hand and with your left hand hold the other rope. That would help, but when you walked, the two buckets would start a backward and forward motion that would splash the liquid all over you.

It is very dangerous when your liquid is coming from the bingo, that is, the slit trench. Using the Yaho pole and buckets was our only way to clean it out. So, learning the koolie trot was a must. You take very small, fast steps forward. No quick stops. Now to do this the wrong way meant you would be covered all over with a bad odor on top of the bad odor you already had for not taking a bath for six months.

There was a rumor that we Americans would be sent to a different camp. Commander Callahan told us that they were going to pull him out and send him to a camp where they kept officers. That was bad news for us because he had proven to us that he was an all-American officer. We hoped the transfer would be good for him. When he became the ranking officer in our group, everyone was treated the same, no matter what. He had proven that when he stood up for all men against the Japs. He stepped out front to take whatever came and never complained once to my knowledge. That was more than you could say about other officers. One time on the ship ride to Japan, a captain started to buck the chow line and Commander Callahan went to him and tapped him on the shoulder. "Hey, to the back of the line like everyone else. Let me remind you that we are all POWs now."

We were now close to the end of our first year in Japan. The winter 1942-1943 was a rough one for most of us coming out of the tropics into such cold weather with light clothes and little food to help keep our bodies warm. We remained cold all winter. If a person cut or hurt his hand, it would not even bleed.

When I joined the Army I had perfect teeth. Now they were getting bad. I had a back wisdom tooth that had to be pulled. They took me to a dentist. When I walked up to his dental chair, I noticed all his tools that were laid out on a glass top table had water circles around them.

He was a very small doctor. His chair was close to the floor. He did not give me anything to deaden my gums. He took a knife that did not look like a dental tool, opened my mouth and just cut all around the bad tooth, stuck some kind of packing in my mouth and let me sit for awhile. Then he came back with his tooth pliers. When he tried to pull the tooth he could not get it out. So he put one foot on the chair armrest, the other foot on the seat beside me. When he pushed down the pliers went against my lower jaw. When he pushed down again the tooth came out, but my jaw also came out of its socket. This was very painful. When I asked him what he was going to do about my jaw he said the American doctor would fix it back at camp.

When I got back, Commander Callahan went to see the old colonel to complain about this type of treatment. We worked my jaw back into place. A thought came back to me as I remembered how my dad pulled our old mule's teeth on the farm.

Some of us were used as experiments while in sick bay. I guess they figured we were going to die anyway. We were never told what the purpose was for the experiment or what effect it would have on us.

We had so many problems that another one did not matter.

While at Osaka #1, I didn't make too many close friends because of my sickness and the bayonet wound, plus the problem with my tooth. But the time I had alone gave me some time to think how to get along with these Japs. They kept telling us that we would not return to the U.S.A. and that our government did not want us back. They also told us that we should learn Japanese and decide that we would have to adjust to the labor details.

Yet my thoughts were more about going back home now. Nothing they told me would make me think that the U.S. government would not allow us to return home. If I had not received the Red Cross box from home, I might have believed them in weak moments even though many things we were told in the Philippines were not the truth.

Even when they tried to get information from us by beating, starving us, even when they tried putting wire under my toenails and getting the wire hot, which gave me great pain, I did not give them any information. Breaking was not for me, even when they threatened the firing squad. If it took stealing food to keep my health and fight off sickness, and taking any treatment they decided to give me, I was determined that they would have to kill me to get rid of me. Now I decided that it was my job to behave and stay out of their way. I would do nothing that might cause them to single me out again, but still work with our small group to destroy anything we could to harm their war effort.

We knew nothing about how the war was going except it was lasting much longer than most expected it to. I would think about what Howard Leachman had said about this was going to be a long ordeal. Sometimes we would see a newspaper that showed some sea battles close to Japan. This gave us some hope. How wonderful it would be to know what was happening, but there was no way to really know what was going on. Even the natives were kept in the dark.

We were told that the Americans would be leaving Osaka #One Camp within a week. We could only hope that our conditions would improve.

— 9 —

Tanagawa

SOME TIME IN THE middle of 1943, the Japs moved all the Americans out of the Osaka #1 Camp across the bay to a village by the name of Tanagawa. Our living quarters were of the same design as those in the Osaka #1 Camp. On the same day that we arrived at the new camp, 225 Americans came in from the Umeda Bucho camp. In all there were 335 of us. The next morning we were all taken to a job site. It appeared that they were building three very large dry docks on the side of a hill. From the look of it, they had been working on the project for some time.

As we lined up, we were put into groups and assigned a Jap *honcho*. Some of the guards at Osaka came with us, along with some guards from Umeda Bucho. We quickly gave them all names—the project boss was Hitler, and Mussolini was a group boss. Another of the guards we called Sir Baloney Bird. These names reflected the way the guards looked and acted.

It turned out that these dry docks were to be used for large ship repair. The walls were being covered with granite rocks polished like diamonds to a beautiful finish. A few husky Koreans had racks on their backs and would load one rock into the rack, take it up walkways and ladders to drop it in location for the next cement run that would hold the rock in place. The Koreans could carry only one piece of granite at a time because of its weight and size. We Americans, as weak as we had become, could never carry even one.

There was a large cement mixer that mixed all the cement for the project. Small cars ran on narrow gauge railroad tracks that extended throughout the job site, carrying cement and other supplies. These cars were also used to carry the dirt and rocks to a boat ramp that extended out over the water so that a barge could come alongside the ramp. The small cars could then dump the rocks and dirt onto the barge to be carried out into the bay and be dumped.

In each dry dock all the dirt and rock being excavated had to be loaded onto the cars. The tracks ran down to the bottom. There was a winch at the top and a cable would be hooked to the last car. The winch operator would lower eight or ten cars at a time for loading. The flagman at the top would tell the winch operator when to pull up the cars. The POWs would then push the cars (two men per car) around the track to the boat ramp and dump the dirt and rocks onto the barge. There were other jobs for us, but this was our main function while on this project.

On one side of us was a prison camp for convicted felons. The inmates there had been doing a lot of work on the project. On the other side of the project the Japanese were building small submarines, and a few were visible. When the workers got them far enough along, they would knock out the blocks under the keel and slide the small submarine into the water and finish it as it floated. Then they would tow them away for final fitting out.

At this time, there were rumors of American B-29s making raids on Tokyo, but up to this point none of them had flown over us. I hoped to see them. The day they flew over us was going to be a happy day for us, even though we knew we were in a dangerous place.

It didn't take long to get to know some of the other Americans who joined us there. I hadn't made many close friends at Osaka #1 Camp, but I did think it would be important to have some friends here. The first POWs I met were Ralph, Roger, (Sam) Clyde, and Mack. We got to know each other well.

There were some POWs who tried to get friendly with the Japs and would do anything for favors. These men would even inform on other American prisoners and caused some of us to be beaten nearly to death. These men were put on notice by us, for what little good it would do. Even one of the officers with us was what we called a "Jap lover."

Our first day at work was not a smooth one. Many men were slapped around or had to stand and hold a piece of railroad iron over their heads. We soon realized that this camp was no better than any other place. There was constant yelling for us to hurry up, to work faster in an effort to pit one American crew against another. That's why it was so important for us to stick together. For example, if there were five cars on one sidetrack, every crew on each car worked at the same speed loading it. If a crew was sick or unable to work fast and another car behind it was loaded up more quickly, it was kept waiting. At that point, the Japs would start hollering. Sometimes a Jap would beat the sick crew that couldn't keep up.

The more work you did, the more they wanted you to do. The Japs were never satisfied. They wanted us to work hard and fast to finish this project so they could use it to repair ships that our submarines were damaging. But there was no way I would work hard, hungry, and half-sick as I was, to help them when they treated us like animals.

We were all getting adjusted to the new place, and discovered we were dealing with a different group of Japanese. Every two weeks our military guards would change. We hated to get new ones because most had been in combat and were delighted to take their anger out on us.

Sometimes they came to our barracks, as many as five or six during the night. They would get us up because our shoes were not lined up straight, just to keep the pressure on us. I never knew when my time would come to be pulled out and beaten for no good reason. I did not expect to live through this punishment anymore than anyone else, but neither did I want to put my life in unnecessary danger. We all felt our lives were at risk twenty-four hours a day.

WORKING WHILE LOADING and pushing the cars on narrow gauge rails always presented the possibility of getting hurt. In fact, one of our guys got his left foot smashed around the ankle area, so they took him to a hospital. When he came back, the Jap doctor had cut his leg off at the hip joint, making it impossible for him to ever have an artificial leg.

Another problem for us was that all the men had diarrhea and it was a problem to go to the *benjo* (toilet). There were only three places the POWs could relieve themselves on the big projects, so most of the time there was a long line. The Japs would see that some of the work was stopped because the workers were lined up to go to the benjo. So they would go to the line, start yelling and telling each man that he did not have to go. Anyone who the Jap told he didn't have to go, would start pulling down his pants to go where he stood. That would cause the Jap to say "no, no," and he would walk off in disgust. We managed to slow work down many times this way. We would do anything we could to slow the work down!

To our surprise, one morning about 10:30 a.m. the air raid alarm went off. Soon we heard high-flying bombers in the distance. We also heard some Zeros in the area. That day high clouds covered most of the sky. However, within twenty minutes the sky was buzzing with the noise of Jap planes. We also started hearing machine guns. Now we were sure that the Jap Zeros were firing on the B-29s. We could also hear what we thought was a different sounding machine gun that came from the high-flying bombers.

Minutes later we heard what sounded like a plane diving. The Japs were jumping up and down, saying, "B-29, B-29." We did not see what kind of plane it was, but it fell not far away. We could hear the plane hit the ground. Soon some smoke came over the top of the hill behind which the plane had crashed. All the time this was going on every American was full of joy, but no one made a sound. We knew they would do something to us if we showed any pleasure that American planes were bombing Japan. On our way to camp we had to go over the hill. When we looked in the direction of where the plane crashed, we could see the tail section sticking up from the ground and on it was a big, red rising sun. Then the guards got real mean, disappointed that the crashed airplane was one of their own. That night we got very little sleep. The guards came into our barracks several times getting us up and counting us as if we were planning to escape. The next day the guards told us how to take shelter when an air raid happened.

Roger was one of the winch operators or flagmen at the top of one of the dry docks where POWs were loading dirt and rocks. If the Japs were not right there watching between the winch operator and the flagman, these workers would hook the last car to the cable so when the last car went over the top the pin would jump out, letting all the cars rush down into the pit tearing up the tracks and dismantling most of the cars. That trick would cause a couple of hours' delay.

The same technique could be used when the cars were being pulled out of the pit after being loaded. When the first car went over the top hump, the pin would jump out and all the loaded cars would plunge to the bottom, tearing most of them up. Once while the damage caused by of one of our sabotages was being repaired, Hitler was standing up on top yelling at everyone. He was standing inside a loop on the winch cable that was on the ground, and the winch operator saw him standing there. He said nothing to anyone, but let the cable, which went up to a portable boom, tighten around Hitler's legs and feet, turning him upside down then dropping him several feet on his head. He was taken away to the hospital.

It was done so slickly that they didn't know if the winch operator knew what he had caused to happen. The first thing the operator did was stop the winch and go over to the crowd of Japs and say he was sorry. They stood him at attention, slapped him around and made him hold a piece of railroad iron over his head until he dropped. Then they kicked him. It was the same old thing they liked to do.

My knee where I was bayoneted in Osaka #1 Camp still bothered me. The weather was also turning cold, and I felt like my malaria was coming back. So I asked for light detail work. This type work consisted of a detail of about ten to fifteen men cleaning up around the project and around the area where the small submarines were being built. There was a fence there where old Japanese women and some children came to watch what was going on. They would come close to the fence and talk to us POWs. They gave us some parched beans that we split up among us.

One of the guys who didn't care about anyone but himself somehow got on the detail. He was not sick but was there anyway. He saw an old lady motioning for someone to come to the fence. She gave him a bag of parched beans. When he came back to the group he refused to split the beans with all the men. He and I got into an argument. Since he was not as sick as the rest of us, he told me that I would have to take them from him, and anyone who thought they could do this should come on.

I stepped up and tried to reason with him but had no luck. Since we were on our lunch break for our rice ball, the guard was not close. He called me a few curse words, and before I could move he hit me pretty hard, knocking me backwards. My right knee gave in and I fell to my knees. A piece of gravel about the size of a marble stuck into the old bayonet wound. The blow caused blood to go everywhere. When the guard came, I told him that I fell, but I told the guy who hit me I would settle with him later.

Our American doctor had no tools to work with and had to fish the gravel out of the wound. He said that the knee was badly bruised, and by the next morning I had a large swollen knee that I could not stand on. I was put in the sick bay where I began running a fever that turned into pneumonia. This was the second time I had had pneumonia in Japan.

Soon the knee got worse. A Jap came by with Dr. Campbell and told him that if it didn't get better soon they would send me to the hospital and take off the leg. I begged Dr. Campbell to please do something, thinking about what they had done to the guy whose ankle got crushed. Dr. Campbell had iodine. By that time the knee was badly infected, so he and I agreed that he would open the wound and try to put pure iodine in it, let it sit for a while, then mash out any infected tissue the iodine would loosen up.

He took a regular pocketknife without anything to deaden my knee, and cut it open while I held a cup to catch the blood and the pus. It was a cold day, but watching the doctor cut on the wound covered me with sweat. This process had to be done every twelve hours. When we saw some green-looking stuff come out of the wound, we knew blood poisoning was setting in. The doctor told the Japs that I was better.

The only place on my leg and knee that had normal flesh was about 1 inch on the back. All the rest of my leg for about eight inches below and above my knee was black and blue. I was in much, much pain, but Dr. Campbell could see some improvement. I stayed in sickbay about 30 days at one time. Out of the twenty-eight men who were there, I was the second sickest one.

One morning someone came in and said they had some soup for us. They started with the sickest patient first. When everyone had been given a cup, they would start over. That's when it sunk into my head that I was in bad shape. When I looked at number one, I knew I had to get out of there. The next day number one died. I could not walk, so I started crawling around the room dragging the old bad knee and leg. Someone asked what the heck I was doing. My reply was I wanted to go back to work. That's when the rest called me crazy, but three days later #3 died. By then I was pulling up and trying to stand on my leg. It took me another month to get well enough to go back on the sick detail that cleaned up the area.

As we watched the Japs who worked on the submarines, we started talking about what would happen if we loosened the blocks that kept the unfinished submarine from sliding down into the water. Every time we got close enough, we would bump the blocks a little. We did this while the riveting guns were making their noise, trying not to make enough noise that the ones working inside the submarine could hear us bumping the blocks. We did this several times. Then one morning when we came to work, our submarine was out in the bay bottom up.

After I reached the point where I could hobble, they put me back on the loading cars where we dug out dirt and rocks from the side of the hill. One day the tugboat taking the dumpster barge out in the bay was late coming back. So all the POWs loaded their cars and pushed them to the boat ramp. After that, we could sit down and wait.

The Japs were not looking, so we pushed all the cars we could onto the ramp butt to butt, to see how many we could put on the ramp before it fell in. We put every car there was room for either back to the bank or where the ramp hooked onto the land.

The dock cracked, but still held up. The last car we had was pushed hard and hit the car in front of it causing all the cars to move a notch. That's all it took. The dock went into the bay—cars, tracks and all. That's when we found out what real beatings were all about. Every man got it. Then they made some of the men get into the cold water and start getting the pieces out of the water. That slowed the entire project down until they could rebuild the dock. We all expected them to shoot us.

There was a huge dirt shovel in front of our camp. It was like a steam shovel on tank tracks. We assumed it was to be used on the project somewhere. It was fully electric. We were told that it came from England. In fact, we could see the name and English writing on it.

On one of our cleanups around the camp, a guy who was a navy electrician got into the control box when the guard couldn't see him and cross-wired it. When they decided to move it, smoke suddenly came out of it and the big motor died. Well, there it sat the rest of the time we were there.

Our "stealing anything of value" program was still working—wire wrenches, tools, just anything we could hide and bring into camp would be thrown into our slit trench in the benjo. Soon the Japs called for a honey wagon (that's what we called it) to clean out our slit trench. When they got into it they found all these items.

They spread them all out and made us walk by so they could pick out who had stolen what. No one would pick out anything, so again we all got a lesson on the evil of stealing and destroying things of value. No one told on anyone else. We all stuck together.

The cement for the mixer was brought into the project by a wagon that was pulled by a big ox. The Jap who drove the ox would yell at it and beat it unmercifully. One day the wagon had a big load on it. The ox stopped and would not or could not pull the wagon up a small incline. With all the yelling and beating, he still would not move. So the Jap unhooked the ox from the wagon, tied him to a tree, and went over the hill talking to himself. Soon he returned with a bigger ox, hooked him up to the wagon and over the hill the wagon went. Soon the Jap returned to where the first ox was tied to the tree. He took the ox's head, tied it sideways tight to the tree. He got out his lunch box and sat right in front of the ox and ate his lunch. He told the ox he was not going to get anything to eat because he did not pull the wagon over the hill. We all could relate to how the ox felt. I'm sure he understood as much as we did when we first were captured and could not understand or figure out what the Japs were capable of doing.

By this time American B-29s were regularly hitting places like Osaka, Kobe, and other cities around us. We were happy to see the bombing, but now realized that we might become targets as well. There was no way the Americans could know where the Japs had the POWs. All we wanted was to see the Japs get what we thought they deserved. They had no mercy on us, so why should they be given mercy?

My friend Clyde was sick some, and like most of us, fed up. With no end in sight, he wondered how long he could last or when his time would come to get beaten to death. Now maybe bombs would kill him. He told me he was thinking about trying to take a gun away from a guard and kill as many Japs as he could before they killed him. I, for one, had at times thought the same, and I knew just how he felt. But at that time I was getting better, and thought I might try to talk him out of it. For about a week every chance I could I would talk to him about it. I also watched him much of the time in case he decided to carry out his threats toward the Japs. It took a good two weeks to change his thinking so he'd realize that maybe we would survive and go home.

I would think many times about what Howard Leachman had told me on the Tayabas Road detail and his premonition that I was the only one he knew who would get back to the USA. I did not have the answer as to how, but that prediction kept coming back to me. This thought gave me hope, which was the only thing I could cling to. I tried to get Clyde to think that way, too. Finally, for some reason, he gave up on his plan.

Another friend, Roger, was always full of hope and looked like he was managing as well as anyone. When some of the men tried to divide us up by pitting one group against another, Roger told them he wanted no part of it. He said his friends were going to stay his friends; he said, too, that this was no time to create faction among ourselves because the Japs were the real cause of all our problems. Whatever their game was, Roger did not play it with them. I have always admired him for that and the many other good qualities he had.

Then there was Ralph, a fellow Alabamian. He and I would sit when we could and talk about what we were going to cook up and eat when we came home. Even a bowl of chitlins sounded good at this point. He could make a steak sound so good that I could just about taste it. He would call me a fellow "hog poler." When I asked him what a "hog poler" was, he said in northern Alabama in the hills there were not many fields to feed the hogs, so they would put them on a pole and hold the hog up against the hill so they could eat what acorns they could find on the side of the hill.

My friend Mack was always there to help anyone. He was from Arkansas. He could do almost anything, but for the Japs he was one of the cooks who didn't know anything but cooking. I do not believe he could boil water without burning it. But he was a true believer that somehow we would all get out. I guess he hated the Japs as much as any of us.

At this time, we had the project as messed up as we could without getting shot. Now the biggest caper of all was trying to get a large rock into the hopper to the big cement mixer. If we could manage to do this, the project would no doubt close for a while. The rock would break the blades that mix the cement and they would have to be replaced. The size of rock needed was hard for us to lift, but we had to do it. To get the rock all the way across the project and into the hopper was a job that took over two months. One time a Jap put the rock back into a car, but by luck we were able to get it out and start it back toward the mixer area.

In the meantime the Japs were starting to pour the cement locks for the front of the dry docks. Now we had to do everything we could to mess up the cement that went into the forms. The forms held the doors that, in turn, held back the water pressure from the bay when a ship was being repaired inside. These doors were about eight feet thick and reinforced with steel, so to weaken the cement we had to put wood, trash, sand or other things to make the cement crack when pressure was put on it. We also knew that the things we added to the cement couldn't show, so that when the forms were removed, the cement still would look good and smooth. We decided that when the cementing started, we had to create a diversion by attacking each other. We could then throw some of the things in and cover them up before they could see what we had done.

As we got close to finishing the first forms, the Japs were building

149

the forms for the other locks. We hoped we could get the rock into the sand hopper before we had to start on the other forms. The Jap prisoners next door told one of our men that they had been working on the project for over ten years. The guards over there treated them about the same as they treated us. Many times we would hear screams coming from their camp.

ALMOST DAILY NOW WE could hear the American B-29s coming closer to us. Many times they would fly over so we could see them. They looked as though they were 50 or 60 thousand feet high. Word was that they were burning out towns and killing many women and children. That was good news for us. We figured it would just be a matter of time before the B-29s would hit this project.

But the Japs were masters at keeping news from us and also from the general population. Most of the working class didn't know much more than we did except that they were being told that the Japanese were winning. But when new army guards came, we sensed things were getting bad by the way they treated us. Once in awhile the guards would refer to the B-29s as being very bad for them.

We had to be very careful whom we told about the rock we were trying to get across the project. There was one American officer who we knew would tell the Japs if he found out. It was a good day when we got word that the rock was now in the hopper in the right place to go straight to the mixer. We couldn't wait! It looked as if it would never get there. Then about 3 p.m. the company whistle blew. That meant assembly time for the POWs. The Japs were buzzing around. The POWs who hadn't received word as to what was happening, asked what was going on. No one that knew would tell them.

It was about quitting time when we got to our camp. All the guards were out along with all the Jap bosses. They had no way to tell if we had done this or not. The man at the cement hopper was there as we lined up and the Jap commander was there. They made us stand at arm's length from each other and then began questioning some of the men. This time, we needed to stick together.

I heard one POW say it was not fair to kill all of us for what a few might have done. As the Japs tried to find out who did this, we all took the position that we knew nothing. The Americans that had nothing to do with it were telling the truth. The ones who did it certainly were not going to tell anything. The Japs lined us up until 11 p.m. There was no dinner rice.

Many men were beaten and some taken into the commander's office. A few of the men who knew the truth were questioned. The rest of us were praying that they did not spill the beans, and thank God, no one gave in and told on the others. I'm glad we were not there when the locks were tested.

Around the end of 1944 we were moved to a graphite factory in Kobe. It was a happy day when we left the rock pile.

Thoughts of an ending of some kind were far from my imagination; after all, I had already been a POW for about three years, but I had been a slave for the equivalent of a lifetime of horrors, killings, beatings, and sickness—all without proper care.

Starvation had become a way of life. I reached the point of expecting nothing and being thankful for just being alive for another day. It seemed as though I had never lived a free life, that being free was a dream that might never have happened. The only hope I had was that America would kill all the Japs by bombing and that maybe some way some of us could escape. The B-29s were our only hope, and if I did not survive, I would be satisfied that the Japs got what they deserved.

We were preparing to go to another camp. All we had to do was grab a handful of things, for that was all we had. I had learned that living was more than material things. Freedom and good health would be a great gift from God if ever again I got the chance to enjoy them.

— 10 —

Kobe Graphite Factory

WE HAD NO IDEA WHERE we were headed as we loaded onto trucks, then transferred to a train. Our guards were very careful not to tell anyone where the train was going. When we arrived at our final destination, we could see big factories all around us. Had we been able to read Japanese, we might have known we were in Kobe. Our concern about B-29s hitting the rock pile was nothing compared to this place with all its factories—just the kind of targets B-29s would like.

When I looked at Roger and Clyde, I knew they were thinking the same thing. There was an airstrip in front of the building where we were unloaded and huge factories all around us. This location is a sure target, I thought. I hoped our barracks would be at a safe distance from this part of our new headquarters, but it was not. We were taken to our new living quarters that were a part of the big building by the airstrip. I thought to myself if this place were to be bombed day or night, we would be sitting ducks. As I looked at each man's face, I could see the disappointment. We all thought the same thing.

Our food was about the same as before, and we even kept the same civilian guards. How I wished we could get rid of the one we called "the emperor." He had at one time or other beaten just about every man for no good reason at all. I think he took out his personal frustration on us POWs. Sir Baloney Bird was not as bad as long as we addressed him as Sir Baloney Bird. When we called him that, he would throw back his shoulders and sort of strut as if he were someone important. I never knew what he thought we were saying.

When we went to work the next morning we were surprised at what we would be making. The building was full of different sizes of extruders to produce graphite cores for dry cell batteries. I soon realized that the large ones were for suicide submarines. Here we were, I thought, directly responsible for making part of a weapon whose purpose was to kill other Americans. This fact bothered all of us.

When the graphite cores came out of the extruder, some were soft and had to sit and cure. Most of the larger cores were hard. An inspector would mark them as good or bad, and the bad ones would go back to be recycled. The good ones went to an area to be stacked for shipping. With this much handling by the POWs, we were able to damage some of the good ones. If they shipped the ones we had sabotaged, the cores could not be used. We soon discovered a few more ways to slow down this production. Since there was no inspection after the first one, we would wipe out the approval markings put on by the inspector and put the batteries into the defective bin. We cut production by fifty to 100 batteries the first month.

DAY AND NIGHT THE B-29s were coming closer and closer. Everyone was concerned about the possibility of being hit. That made it important to figure out how we were going to get out of this place.

With graphite everywhere around us, each of us began to look as if we had been painted black. There was not enough soap to get it off and some of the men would use sand as sandpaper on their skin. That would take off some of the graphite, but the men still kept getting blacker. One day one of the guys had what the doctor thought was a stroke or epilepsy attack. He was foaming at the mouth, kicking, and rolling on the ground. None of the Japs would get close to him. They told our cook to put him in sickbay. When they asked what was wrong, we told them he had a tropical disease and that it was contagious. This little episode gave us a way to get out of there—that is, if they thought they might catch it. We noticed that the guards would not go into the sickbay anymore.

We found out, too, that one of the buildings was full of wheat. In addition, we figured out a way to cook it by pulling up floorboards and putting a can of charcoal between the floor and the ground. This way a small amount of wheat could be prepared. It was hard, though, to get into the storage building to steal the wheat. Mack and I discovered a way to get past the guard, who had to walk from one side of the building to the other. When he turned to go away from us, we would run across the drive to the backside of the building with the wheat and go through a window. Then we would make our way back across the drive and stash the wheat for a later pickup.

As we crossed the drive the guard saw us and ran towards us. Mack went in one direction and I went in another. The guard was following me. I ran around a building, and just as I turned the corner I saw five POWs digging a small drainage ditch. One of the workers had gone to the benjo and a shovel was lying on the ground. I grabbed it up and started digging. When the Jap came around the corner I pointed to another building. He took off running, I dropped the shovel and went back to my job, only to get slapped for taking so long at the benjo. Later when we cooked the wheat we found that the wheat was soaked with napalm from a recent B-29 attack. It made us sick. One guy ate some and swelled up twice his size. His belly stuck out so far he could not stoop over. We kidded him, telling him not to point his rear at us!

One night the B-29s came so close we could hear the bombs explode and could see that an area not far from us was on fire. That's when we decided we had to get out of there. We decided we would all start having seizures, but not too many at the same time. Someone came up with faking a hanging one night. The guards asked why the man hanged himself. We told them that he was starting to get the tropical disease like the POW that was foaming at the mouth. They became scared of that and would not touch this POW.

By now the battery production was down from 300 a month when we arrived to fewer than 100 a month. The Japs were getting upset and took all the POWs away from the machines. They also started making more inspections to see if we were damaging the sticks, but by now we could still do the same things, just in different ways. They did not have sufficient inspectors to keep us from damaging batteries to keep the production numbers down. The guards would knock us around. Most of the time we would act crazy. They did not know what to do with us. Someone told them the tropical disease made us act that way. A couple of months before, the POWs had started having seizures. The Japs were also told that the building was not healthy to work in and may have caused the sickness.

At the end of three months they thought we were all going crazy. The production was down to nothing, and we had become useless to them. At this point, the Jap workers were afraid to work with us; so once again, we were told that we were going to be moved.

The morning we lined up to go, a marine who could understand Japanese heard two Japs talking and they expressed the view that maybe we were putting on a lot of this, but it was too late because the Jap workers wanted us gone.

— 11 —

Tsuraga

FROM KOBE WE WERE sent to Tsuraga, our fourth camp since our arrival in Japan as POWs in November, 1942. Although the camp locations differed, the conditions remained the same. All the winters were cold and the summers almost unbearable. In every camp we suffered severely without proper food, housing, medicine, or clothing, both winter and summer.

It is hard to believe that any of us survived this harsh way of living. Our bodies were still alive, but our minds were numb. We stumbled through each day trying not to think about our situation. We did our best to make ourselves believe that we were not hungry, or hurting, or living without one moment of privacy. The only privacy allowed was in our thoughts, and each of us tried to stay away from the darker places in our minds. We needed the company of each other to reassure ourselves that we were still alive.

Each one of us had been beaten many times. It was hard to accept the fact of being beaten. I do not mean just the indignity of having to stand there knowing you cannot do anything to protect yourself or you will die, not just the suffering and pain you feel as a rifle butt connects with your head, or your stomach, or anywhere on your body, but the feeling you have of total helplessness. You stand there wanting to spit on your attacker, wanting so badly to put both your hands around his neck and squeeze until all the frustration has gone out of you and the life out of him. You imagine killing the enemy, planning how you can inflict the most pain or spill the most blood, but most of all wanting to see the eyes of your enemy reflect surprise, pain, and the ultimate realization that *he is going to die-* and that *you are the one who will kill him.*

Seeing others getting beaten is almost as bad as if it were happening to you, especially if the victim is sick or too weak to make it through another attack. You feel each blow, the mental and physical pain of the victim, and a total outrage that the attacker does not or will not acknowledge the weakness or illness of the person he is attacking. It is the lack of feeling on the part of the person doing the beating that got to us most. We never became accustomed to the totally inhuman way that the beatings were administered, as if we were totally without the ability to feel pain.

We were entering into our third year as POWs. Most of us were wondering if we would ever live to see the end of this terrible war. I felt hopeless and could not think of any way to get out alive. Most of the men had the same feelings and asked the same question, "Why did I fight to survive this brutal treatment if after all my suffering the end result is death?" I could not see any way to defeat the Japs except for our forces to invade their homeland, at which time we would all surely be killed.

Our only hope of winning the war came from seeing that the B-29s were still bombing Japan, and that the Japanese were showing the effects of it. We prisoners knew first hand how seemingly endless bombing will sooner or later overwhelm you. The Japanese were suffering from the strain of the daily threat of danger, destruction, and the feeling that they might die during the next bombing raid. We did not feel sorry for them.

We were marched to the railroad station, leaving to go to our new camp at Tsuraga. There we were loaded on a train. A Jap came out the door of the station as we walked by and asked in English how many men there were, where we came from, and where we were going.

It made us feel good to think our government might know more about the POWs in Japan than we had thought. Until now we all felt that maybe Tokyo Rose, talking to us over the radio back in Bataan, was right in telling us we might not be welcomed back to the USA. After all we have been through, physically and mentally, it was easy for our minds to drift into doubt as to whether the people back home still cared about us. Three years of slavery had been a long time—long enough to feel unloved and unwanted by everyone, including our own families back home.

My thoughts about home were not the same as they had been during the first part of the war. When I was first captured I thought about my girlfriend, my family, and my childhood friends as they had been when I left them. Now three and a half years had passed. Not only would they have changed, I myself had changed. I began to think about not going home at all. If they have received word that my dog tags had been found in the mass grave at Camp O'Donnell, why should I give them more grief? I should just go somewhere else and let them believe my life had ended at Camp O'Donnell.

Soon the train we were riding in entered a valley. I could see a port that looked like an out-of-the-way place surrounded by mountains. It looked like a peaceful place, and I had a sudden rise of hope that we were coming to a place that would give us the possibility of ending this horrible ordeal as prisoners.

This town was smaller than Osaka or Kobe. We were close to the seaport, and I could see ships in the harbor. My first thought was that maybe we would be unloading ships from Manchuria. If so, there was a possibility of handling food, and we might be able to smuggle some of it into camp. What would it feel like to have a full stomach for a change, being able to say, "No more, thank you. I've had plenty to eat?"

When we arrived at our new quarters we found the living conditions the same as before. The camp commander gave us the same old speech, "Obey orders or be punished. You are a guest of the emperor while here in Japan." I sure would have hated to be there as a slave.

Our rice ration was about the same as that at the other camp, soggy with a few black-eyed worms. We brought along our body lice to keep us company. I thought back to the time when our interpreter had told us back in Tanagawa that he didn't want us "sleeping with the bear" and "making trouble with the fleas."

Our civilian guards were still with us—the Emperor and Sir Baloney Bird. I now weighed about 125 lbs., and still walked with a limp in my right leg from the bayonet wound I had received from a Jap guard.

The date was sometime in January, 1945. The north wind coming off the water was chilling, cutting right through the old Jap uniform I had been given to wear. The cement paper we had used before to stop the wind from freezing us to death was about worn out and helped very little to keep us warm.

WHEN WE LINED UP for work assignment the first morning in the new camp, all of us had high expectations that maybe we would be unloading ships. Sure enough, we were marched right down to the docks where several ships were tied up. There, we met our new Japanese bosses. One who acted more important than the others was a Jap about five feet nine inches tall with long legs and a short body. It didn't take long to name him Bird Legs. The other boss looked a little simple-minded. He was wearing a baseball cap with the bill turned up. Before long we named him Simple Simon.

The bosses separated us into groups of twenty to thirty men. My first job was cleaning up the mess in a long warehouse along the dock. There was room for about four ships to dock at one time. As far as I could determine, the ships were loaded with bags of rice, soybeans, and boxes of dried fish. Some of the ships were also carrying machinery and steel railroad irons.

There was a railroad siding running the length of the warehouse. Some men began to carry bags of beans and rice from the ship and stacked them in the warehouse ready to load into railroad cars. There were some beans and rice spilled on the floor, and we were told to scoop them up and put them in a can that looked like a garbage can. We were told not to eat any beans or rice that if we did we would be punished. Within minutes I had a mouthful of raw beans. You just couldn't let a Jap see you chewing. If a Jap asked you a question while you were trying to chew the beans, you had to swallow the beans whole to answer him.

The first day passed without many problems, but getting to know our new bosses took a little time. If a prisoner asked about the B-29s and whether there had been any damage from them, he was slapped a few times and told, "No B-29s in Tsuraga." We were glad to hear that good news for our own safety.

Soon our new interpreter came around. He spoke to us in good enough English so that we could understand him, but he actually had very little to say to us. When we got back to the barracks that night, the interpreter told some of the men that he was American-born also from Cleveland, Ohio. He told us that he and his family had come to Japan to see some family members before the war, and the Japanese government had kept them from returning to the United

States. We soon found out the Japs didn't trust this interpreter, and most of the time he had a guard following him around whenever he was close to us. This was the first interpreter who had shown any interest in our condition and in how we were getting along. He said he had very little influence with the Japs and was limited as to what he could do, but would help us whenever he could.

He showed no interest in having a guard beat us just because he had that power over us. This made all of us feel a little better. He later told us our delay-and-destroy program was going to be a snap to put into place here. We soon realized that this inland port, though small in size, was a very important one for supplying food to all of Japan. All we had to do now was decide how we could slow down the flow of food.

Our main plan was to make anything we did look accidental. As soon as you did something, you should run tell the Jap guard or boss, "*Sumie my sin*," meaning, "I'm sorry," to allay their suspicions. At first our plan worked well, but soon there had been too many "accidents," and the guards watched us more closely.

One of the Japanese bosses came to us and had the interpreter tell us that they wanted any navy men who were available to run the winches that pulled the nets of bags out of the hold of the ship and move them to the dock side of the warehouse. He said they wanted to relieve the Jap winch operators so they could go on to help the rest of the Japanese Army. That was the worst thing they could have told us. We sure didn't want to relieve anyone so they would be free to help fight our men.

All the men told the Japs that they were navy cooks. In the end, they made four of the men get on the ships and showed them how to operate the winches and booms. When the first American tried to unload the first net he pulled it up all the way to the top end of the ship's boom. Then he started moving it from side to side, and let the net down about half way. The heavy net kept swinging from side to side and broke one of the side ropes, letting a bag sling all the way out over the water. When the net went swinging toward the warehouse, two bags of food came out of the net like a missile, shooting one bag through the roof of the warehouse. The other bag hit the side of the warehouse and burst, with the rice going all over the place. About five Japs began yelling. Before they could stop it, the net hit the ship's rails, tearing them down. The balance of the load from the net went back down in the hold of the ship with a big bang.

When they finally got the POW away from the winch controls, he told them he was a cook and did not know how to run a winch. They gave him a good beating. The other men showed similar problems with operating the winch. One pulled the net to the top, mashing the clutch and letting it freefall back into the ship's hold. It just about knocked the bottom out of the ship. That incident was the end of the navy men running the winches.

Bird Legs told us that we had a sorry navy. He said all Jap sailors knew how to run winches. He also said American cooks did not know how to cook rice.

We had some Japs who worked alongside us. They all wore belly bands to keep their stomachs warm, but they also put rice and beans inside the belly band each day to take home. However, they helped the Army guards check us when we left to go to barracks at the end of the day. When they searched us and found rice or beans in our pockets we would touch their belly band and say, "*momeys*" (beans).We would be looking straight at the Jap. He knew that we knew he was also stealing, and that he would be severely punished if he were caught. So he would just pass on down the line and not report anything bad about us to the Jap guard. This way we all got rice and beans into the

163

camp. It helped the sick get a little more food, and we would all eat raw rice or beans after our meager ration of cooked rice.

With the extra food, all the POWs started to feel better and began to get into a little better shape. It wasn't long before I was put on the detail of moving bags from the warehouse to the trains. We learned how to carry a bag that weighed over 100 lbs. on our back from the warehouse, up a plank and into the rail car. The Japs were a little better to us on this work detail.

We figured out a way to delay and destroy their food supply in several small ways; we felt that every little bit helped. The railroad cars were small compared to our American cars. They ordered us to load 380 bags in each car. We cut down on this load by piling bags higher at the door than inside the car. The Jap inspector was short. He would come by to inspect by looking in the car from the ground. He would ask us, "380 bags?" We would answer," Hei," meaning, "Yes." The inspector would then close the door, put the car seal over the door lock and go to the next car.

Now to make it look like someone stole from the car after it left the yard we would cut the seal off before the train pulled the cars out. We never let a car out of the yard with a seal on a car that we had short-changed.

We figured we were destroying some of their food supply, but this success brought on another problem. We were getting stacked up with rice and beans in the warehouse. We would start a fight inside the warehouse to get all the Japs to run inside. Some of us were at the dockside to throw food bags into the bay. This worked for a while, but one morning the tide was out and a couple of ships could not get close enough to pull up dockside.

The Japanese ordered a dredge to come clear out the bay near the dock area, but it took a couple of days to get it there. When it finally arrived and began working, up came bags of beans and rice. The result of that discovery was a big beating for all of us who worked in that area.

Our boss, Simple Simon, was not too swift. We could fool him about many things. One day when we were faking a fight among us to cover up something we were doing, someone hit his baseball cap bill. When this happened, Simple Simon's eyes went up and turned backwards into his head. He had to be led away to the hospital.

Within a couple of weeks Simple Simon returned to work as our boss. As soon as he would start yelling at us, or doing something mean to one of us, we would fake a fight so that we could get close to him and flip his cap bill down. Every time we did that, he was taken away to stay in the hospital for a few weeks. Bird Legs told us to be careful around Simple Simon and to help him when this happened to him. They never figured out that we were flipping his cap bill down, and away he went to the hospital again.

AFTER A COUPLE OF months we began to hear the air raid signal. Sometimes we would hear high-flying planes, but could never spot any. The Japs would say the planes were over the mountains and order us to keep working. Bird Legs had an iron, triangular-shaped device that he would beat on to warn of a raid. If the air raid warning sounded off in short signals, that meant the planes were close and not over the mountains and might be flying over us. Then, if he could see the planes, he would hit three times on his device in three separate signals that alerted us to take cover. Every time the long sounds went off, Bird Legs would go outside to see if he could spot the planes. Our only instructions on air raid warnings were his signals to us.

The first few months at this location were going pretty well. We were getting to eat more beans and rice during the day. Some of us even had stashes in our bed area. We were also stealing anything of value to throw in our benjo just to get rid of it so the Japs could not use it.

Each bunk was marked with a number. My number was 632. One day we were ordered to come back into camp early. To our surprise the Japs had pulled an inspection of all the bunks. If they found anything that you were not supposed to have during the inspection, they removed it and put your number on it.

There were many things displayed on tables. All the men in the sick bay were there as witnesses. You had to go to the table to see which items your number was on. They would take the item with your number, and in front of all the others they would beat you until you could not stand up. Sometimes they would kick you when you lay too helpless to get up. When there were too many men on the floor the Jap guards would drag some of them out of the way. I thought they were going to kill my friend Roger, because he had several items on the table. The next morning they would beat you again if you tried to stay off work that day.

We were unloading narrow gauge railroad tracks that had been shipped in from Manchuria, then reloading them on railroad gondoliers to be shipped out. There was a harsh supervisor in charge of our loading efforts, and he kept yelling at us. Loading the rails was a hard job for us. The boom lifted them up in bundles. Over the side of the gondolier was a small winch that had two ropes on the boom. A man held each rope. When the winch lifted the rails up, one man had to pull the boom over the top of the gondolier. When the winch lowered the bundle onto the gondolier, one man inside would unhook one side, then signal to pull the cable up to get it out from under the rails and clear, ready for another bundle. The other man on the other rope would then pull the boom back to the pile of rails on the ground. When the winch was pulling the cable up, sometimes the rails would shift, and anyone working in the gondolier had to be careful not to get hurt.

One of the Jap guards was not satisfied as to how my friend Mack was working inside the gondolier, so he climbed inside to show Mack how to stack the tracks and keep them straight to make more room for a larger number of tracks to be loaded. He got the winch operator and Mack so confused, a bundle shifted and crushed him into the wall of the gondolier. One of the bands used to connect the rails went into his groin and lower stomach area. We pulled the rails off him.

One of our crew ran and told Bird Legs what had happened. They took the injured Japanese out and laid him on the ground, but the blood was soaking his pants. While waiting for someone to take him to the hospital, the Japanese did not open his pants to try to stop the bleeding. Instead, they tried to look in through a hole the rail had torn into his pants to see how bad the injury was.

When the emergency equipment arrived, it turned out to be a three-wheeled bicycle with a basket on back. They loaded him into the basket with his head hanging over to one side, which happened to be the side next to the railroad tracks. The Japs were all yelling for the bicycle operator to hurry up. He took off as fast as he could with the tires running over the ends of the railroad ties.

As the Japs yelled, this poor man's head was bouncing up and down hanging out of the basket. I think the ride is what killed him, not the loss of blood. To us this dead Jap was just another one who had mistreated us and was now out of the way. At this point we had no mercy for any of them.

We were hearing more frequent air raid warnings, but the planes never seemed to fly over us. Once, when a warning came in the middle of the night, we were expecting the all-clear sound to tell us the danger was all over. But soon the short signals started, warning that the planes were in our area. The guards were trying to pass the word to take us out. Then we heard planes coming close and soon the bombs started coming down. Most of the bombs landed on another part of the town, but our area was being hit, too.

Our barracks soon caught fire, and it was going up in flames along with all the buildings around us. Each of our little handfuls of belongings went up in flames. I thought, "Well, what can you lose if you really have nothing?"

Out of our 340 men only one got burned a little on his face. For the first time the Japs (most of the time it was our guard, Bird Legs) looked at us and said, "Your own country bombed you. Why didn't some of you get hit?" We told Bird Legs that we had been through this before, so we knew where to go and what to do in a bombing. After that the Japs would wait to see where we went during an air raid. You would have to run fast to get in a ditch or trench before three or four Japs would beat you there! I had to lie on top of Bird Legs and two other Japs during one raid.

Our barracks were gone. All you could see were the outlines of the buildings. Ashes covered the ground, and you had to look carefully to see where our building had been. The Emperor came to head up a detail of us POWs to help clean up the area. We all hated the Emperor, so one of our group found an old benjo slit trench and stuck a stick down into it. Then we plotted to get the Emperor straight across from it. The guy then called the Emperor to come see what he had found. The Emperor came walking straight towards him. He walked right into the bingo slit trench and fell in up to his head. He was covered with POW waste. He crawled out yelling and started pulling off his clothes. By the time he got to the water, he was as naked as a jaybird. He was so mad he wanted to kill every one of us.

Our friendly interpreter talked him out of it, saying the man who had summoned him did not know exactly where the bingo slit trench was located. The great Emperor was never the same after that.

OUR SIR BALONEY BIRD was very proud of his name, and many times he would smile and strut when called by it. Then he took a two-week leave. The first formation after he got back we noticed that he was not at all happy with us. After head counting he went to the front of the formation and in broken English he said, "I found out my name, *Sir Baloney Bird* (Jo to ni) meaning 'no good.' Never want to hear again." The interpreter was amused at us and at him. He warned us not to give him a chance to beat us because he might "take the beating to the end"—meaning our death. So we were all very careful after that and never let him hear us call him by his nickname again.

After our building was burned out, they moved us to an abandoned brick kiln on the edge of town across the street from a large clothing factory. The air raids were picking up. The sound would go off every thirty to forty minutes. The planes did not always hit our area, but came close enough.

We talked the Japanese into letting fifty men at a time wash our only clothes in salt water without soap—not very effective, but it gave us a day off. There were fifty of us naked in the end of the long warehouse waiting for our clothes to dry. One of the guys with the artillery unit looked outside because he heard something. He looked through his fingers at the sun and yelled, "Here they come, down 11 a.m."

We did not know what he meant. He said run, run. Fifty men were trying to get through the door next to the railroad tracks at one time. On the other side was a long pile of coal. A guy by the name of Draper and I were the last to get to the door. We looked at forty-eight guys going over the coal pile naked. I fell down laughing. The alarm was for our navy dive bombers. As I looked back I could see fire all over the place, the rockets going in every direction. We made our way to a small hill that overlooked the dock area.

Wave after wave of our navy planes was flying overhead. There was a Jap up in the ship's mast with a machine gun. He was waiting for the planes to pull up after dropping their bomb loads, then he would shoot at them. A navy pilot spotted him and pulled up in a different direction. The Jap jumped out of the crow's nest and landed on the ship's deck. We never saw him move.

We were up there yelling, jumping up and down like we were at a football game. What a wonderful sight. Soon the pilot saw us and realized we were American POWs, so he gave his plane wings a couple of waves at us. After that all the planes pulled up and went out over the port, not over us. I wish I could have heard just what he reported about fifty naked American POWs standing on a hill waving and jumping up and down.

The air raid did a lot of damage to that little port. After that the Japs took off whenever the air raid warnings sounded. Their attitude also got meaner towards us. The interpreter tried to get some of us alone to tell us how he felt. He expressed compassion for us. He delivered some 16mm movies to us to help us understand how long the Japs had tried to turn their children against Americans. In the movies monkeys were used to portray the Imperial Japanese race and white pigs were shown as the Americans, proving to the kids that they were the superior race.

We found out that a combination of rice, onions, and orange peelings would produce a lot of gas, and when we passed this gas, anyone around us would have to leave. We used our malodorous wind like the skunks use theirs against an attacker. If a Jap started at us, any American who had been eating these items would let the Jap have it. In every case, he would leave in a hurry.

As we walked back and forth to the docks, the kids and some adults would scream curse words at us. Kids as young as six or seven years old would run out and try to kick us and spit on us. They would yell that B-29s were "jo to ni" —no good.

By the end of July or the first of August, 1945, American planes were bombing all over Japan. They just kept coming right on schedule, about every thirty minutes. In spite of this, our Jap bosses kept the pressure on us.

ABOUT THIS TIME, I remembered something my mother had told me when I was still a child. She said if you saw the new moon clearly, with no obstruction, depending on how much or what type obstruction was between you and the moon (be it trees, clouds or anything), it showed what kind of a month you would have. In 1941 the new moon I saw in the Philippine Islands was behind trees and clouds. I only saw a small tip of it. I thought, "Oh darn, I'll have a bad month."

Then on December eighth the Japs hit Pearl Harbor and eight hours later, the Philippine Islands. The war was on. I did not see the moon clearly until the end of July, 1945, when I looked up and there it was—as clear as I had ever seen it. My breath was short as I stood there looking at it.

When I went back into the barracks I told everyone that within 30 days we would be dead or free. It would be over. They all told me, "Frazier, you of all people make that statement? You have never said anything like this. Why do you say that now?" I said, "I've seen a sign right from heaven, and it's real. I do not understand it, but that is what will happen."

I thought about what Howard Leachman had told me in the

Philippines on the Tayabas Road detail. It gave me hope to remember that he had said that I was the only one he knew who would make it back to the USA. I had no idea as to how that would happen, because it looked as though an invasion of Japan would be the only hope of ending the war. I couldn't think of any way that we POWs could survive an invasion because these people were so hostile toward us about the extensive bombing. In addition, they were training the old men, women, and children as to how to defend the homeland in case the allied forces invaded Japan.

The navy dive bombers were coming in almost every day. Many times we would see B-29s fly over and also, a couple of times a day, a reconnaissance plane would fly over. The guards and workers were now extremely hostile to us.

Our interpreter was acting more friendly towards us, since the Japs were not watching him as closely. It was reaching the point where they were more concerned about their own safety than about us. Our B-29s and dive bombers would fly in without any Jap planes attacking them. I am not sure if it was that way all over Japan, but it was true of the place where we were.

After they moved us out to the old brick kiln, we were not as afraid of being firebombed, because the building was out in the open. The guards were yelling at us more and waking us up at night for no good reason. They told us if the B-29s came we would have to move out into the rice field. I think they wanted to get out of the building themselves. With them guarding us we did feel a bit safer from the general population, but we had our own plan of defense if the Japs tried anything.

One of the men in our group found a newspaper showing a picture of Okinawa. He said it looked like a battle picture. That helped us understand where all the Navy bombers were coming from. We knew if the Americans were that close our aircraft carriers would also be close enough to send bombers over us. We figured that after the navy pilot saw us the planes would hit the ships and railroad cars, and we tried to stay away from the dock area buildings.

One day we noticed that all the Japs were very upset. Things were not as usual with them. The interpreter came by to tell us that the United States had dropped a bomb so big that it had destroyed a large city. He said if you were seventy-five miles away from where the bomb was dropped and reading a paper, it would petrify you while you were sitting in the chair.

This at first sounded like a big propaganda stunt they were pulling, but if you watched the way the Japs were acting, this rumor did seem to be something different. They took us back to the brick kiln. Nothing was said to us, but we were confined to the inside of the building. A few more guards came to watch us. We knew that with their mood the way it was, we had to stay quiet and keep a low profile.

THE NEXT MORNING WE were awakened by the guards yelling and seeming to be very excited. We were lined up, but not in the same way as if we were going to work. The guards marched us out to the edge of town to an open rice field. Soon a couple of trucks arrived. One was loaded with several new guards and four machine guns. The other truck had picks and shovels loaded on the back.

As they unloaded the trucks it was hard to stand still and wait to see what was up, but one thing we had all learned was to keep our cool until we knew for sure what was going to happen. What first went through our minds was that this was where we were going to be killed and buried.

When all the guards were unloaded, they took a machine gun to each of the four corners of the rice field. We were trying to keep each other calmed down. The guard in charge told us that all POWs were to be killed if and when any allied forces landed on the Japanese mainland. He also warned us against trying to escape. We were there to dig our own graves.

My first thought was that I never figured I would be pushing up daisies in Japan. Somehow we must get out of this. One thing gave us some hope and that was that we didn't think the allied forces were yet ready for the invasion of Japan. We figured there might be a few days to think about what we could do. I thought that if they were going to wait to kill me until I got my own grave dug, I would be the slowest grave digger on record.

So we started digging slowly, talking very low to each other. We had learned how to be masters of the art of being slow, but also how to look like we are digging with the back of the shovel. Time moved slowly by. When noon came we were instructed to leave our tools there because we were going back to camp, then return after noon break.

While we were back in camp each person teamed up with two others, making a team of three persons. The reason for this was that when we knew for certain they were going to shoot us, we would all break loose with our picks and shovels, running as fast as we could trying to take down a machine gun in hopes of killing some of the Japs. If there were a chance of any of us getting away, a group of three men would be the best number to go into hiding someplace. Two could then rest while the other one could watch. This way maybe some of us could survive and reach the American invading forces.

With this plan in place we went back to the rice field. The afternoon was not too bad. A few guys were slapped around a bit for not digging very hard. I guess I must have dug about six inches the first day. We made the digging look really hard for us.

That night many of the guys came close to losing control of their emotions. This was no time to make any mistakes. We were afraid if the guards started shooting for any reason, they would kill all of us. We knew they were capable of doing just that. I considered this group of 340 POWs to be as tough as they come. They had been through three and a half years of slave labor, taken everything these Japs could dish out, and still they were standing face to face with their enemy.

If the killing started, the Japs would have their hands full. I now had gotten my weight up to 165 lbs. and was used to carrying over 100 lbs. on my back for hours at a time. It would be hard for ten Japs with just four machine guns to handle all of us.

As we lay down to rest that night most of the men were very quiet. Now and then you could hear someone crying softly. We all showed how we felt about each other, giving comfort to the ones who needed help and voices of condolence that somehow this would work out, but if not, our plight would finally be over. All the pain, the suffering that we never expected we could endure to begin with—all of it would be done.

The third day of digging our graves began. We were facing the machine guns, not knowing when one or all four would be used to shoot at us. As we fell out to work, I think the Japs knew by looking at us how we felt because they seemed to handle us a little more carefully. The look on each of our faces was stern. We never showed once that we were afraid of them.

Maybe this is the feeling that comes over brave men when the going gets tough. Our graves were still shallow. We did not know how deep they had to be before they would start the shooting, and we did not know what their orders were. So it was stand brave, face our enemy with no emotions, and don't show any sign of fear.

We dug very slowly. At noon, the time came for us to return to the brick kiln. I think every man was making the same assumption that maybe this was the time we would be killed, but all of a sudden the head guard told us to go back to camp. A look of relief appeared on every man's face.

As we walked back down the road to camp, a glimmer of hope came over me. I never figured I would thank God for another day of being a slave for these savage Japs. I was like most of the other men. After being brought up to that high a level of tension then getting a break, the let-down made me feel weak in my knees. Marching between my close, dear friends was the only comfort I could find. I did not think about going home or hope this would end for us as we had dreamed so many times.

Each one of us hated to think about going back to the rice field after our lunch break, because it would bring our feelings of tension right back to the point where we were before lunch. We knew our lives might now be down to counting hours.

Many things were racing through my mind. At the sound of the first shot I was going to go as fast as I could to try to take a machine gun and not only kill the guards, but to go into the streets to shoot the kids that spit, kicked, and even tried to urinate on us as we walked past them in the streets.

Within minutes of our call to fall out, the air raid warning started. It didn't take long before the short alarms started sounding that the planes were in our area. The guards had not put us back inside the building so we were outside where we could see the planes. I felt a flare of anger come over me toward the Japs. Come on B-29s, drop one of those big bombs on these Japs and kill all of them. I would be proud to die by our bombs instead of their bullets.

As we looked we only saw one B-29 flying about 20,000 feet high. It was circling around the valley as if it was looking for something.

Soon it started straight toward us. One of the 200 Coast Artillery guys yelled that the bomb bay door was open and the plane was coming right in on us. There was nowhere to go so we just lay flat on the ground and braced for the bomb that we knew would probably hit us. Someone yelled that the bomb had come out.

Minutes later we heard the shrill noise that we had heard so many times before. The ground shook as the bomb hit the big building across the street. The debris rained down on us. Pieces of wood, shingles, dust and dirt rained down on us. What a relief came over me. I think every man yelled and jumped with joy at the destruction of the building instead of our fragile lives. As the emergency equipment and personnel rushed to the building, we were left alone, locked up in the brick kiln.

What a change in just five minutes. Before lunch we were expecting the Japanese to start shooting us because they were so nervous and delayed our return to the brick kiln at lunchtime. After lunch the interpreter told us to fall out and go back to the rice field. In that five minutes our lives changed forever.

The guards were helping next door. We were told that over 400 workers were killed. The 2000 lb. bomb hit the building exactly where the big smokestack came out of the top—dead center. It took well over a day to clear the debris from the street. The interpreter came the next morning to tell us that the Japanese Emperor was going to talk to the nation. He said that the Japanese and Americans were discussing the war and that, in the meantime, the bombing would stop.

— 12 —

Leaving Japan

THE EMPEROR SPOKE FOR two and a half hours, and we listened on loudspeakers. One of the POWs was a marine who had spent time in China and who had had a Japanese girlfriend and could understand most of the speech. The Emperor told the people that many of them would be killed if the Allied forces invaded the mainland and that it was time to stop the war, time for all civilian and military personnel to lay down their arms and stop the fighting so that the B-29s would not bomb them anymore.

We noticed that our guards had moved out of our building and were posted outside the fence next to the road, including the Emperor (ours, this time) and Sir Baloney Bird. We could also see Japanese soldiers going up the mountain west of us carrying guns and supplies, but we did not know where they were going.

Soon the interpreter came to tell us what to expect. He also asked us to help him and his family by signing a statement saying that he had been fair to us. This would be for his wife and children. So our captain, who was the ranking officer, prepared a letter for him, and all of us signed it. I have not mentioned this captain nor his lieutenant very often because none of us liked them. They did very little to help the men with the Japanese and in some cases caused some of the men to be beaten so badly they never recovered.

What we wanted to do was grab the guards we called the Emperor and Sir Baloney Bird along with about five others, bring them to the brick kiln, put them in the large oven, and burn them to death. But no such luck; they were all gone. The guards that were with us up to the time the bomb hit the building across the street were also gone.

The interpreter came to tell us an agreement of surrender had been approved, that we would be going home, and that the present guards were there to protect us from any Japanese who might want to harm us. I stood there with tears of joy running down my face. It was hard to believe. Just a few days earlier we were digging our own graves and were sure that the only hope of escape was through dying. **Now we were going home. Looking around I could see a strange, surprised and almost unbelieving look on everyone's face.** I never expected it to end this way, but what a blessing. I think it took two days to sink in that our wishes were finally coming true.

They brought us some red, white, and blue cloth and told us to make a simulation of our American flag and put it on top of the building. We were told also to display the number of men in the camp so the American reconnaissance planes could see it, and we would receive an airdrop of food, medicine, and clothes.

What a wonderful feeling we all had. Food, clean clothes, maybe a pair of shoes without holes in them, and medicine for the sick. It was so hard to believe! I think most of us were in shock. We couldn't get the flag made fast enough, and we kept looking for a sign of the reconnaissance plane.

The next day someone spotted a high-flying plane. We all ran out waving and jumping up and down, yelling as if they could hear us. It did us all good and helped us realize that everything that was happening was true. Everyone was wishing for his favorite food and telling each other how they were going to cook it. No one could sleep.

We were all walking around and talking to each other about home and what we were going to do when we got there. I wondered if my girlfriend was still single and if she would still want to see me. I also wondered how I would mend the hurt I caused my family for leaving without telling them where I was until November of 1941. I also wondered how Nelda was doing in the Philippine Islands and if all her family had made it through the war. I would not know how to reach them now. In addition, I was also certain that we would not go back to the Philippines on our way home. There were uncertainties everywhere. We had no idea what the army planned to do with us.

A couple of days passed without getting the promised airdrop. Then one day we saw a B-29 flying low around the valley. We also noticed that a large crowd was forming around our building. The guards kept the townspeople back in the street. The B-29 made a couple of passes over us, and we were all yelling and waving. Just beyond our building was a rice field. The guards were keeping the Japs away from that area so we thought that maybe the drop might be there. On the next pass made, we noticed the bomb bay doors were open. We were yelling, "This is it."

As the 55-gallon welded-together drums came out of the bomb bay, the Japs in the street thought bombs were coming out. This caused a stampede among them, and many were hurt as they ran away. They did not wait to see the parachutes open. The drum with medicine went through the roof into the hospital area. Others went into the rice field and sank into the ground. A few Japanese got past the guards and tried to take some of the things that came out of a couple of burst drums. We thought: "No way!" We knocked them down and sent them packing. Boy, did it feel good to hit a Jap without getting beaten yourself!

We opened the drums as quickly as we could. The captain started his bull about regulations and was choosing certain men to help him take control. Even he could not put a damper on things, and our first meal out of what had been dropped was like a gift from heaven. Everyone was excited. I've never seen any group of little kids opening Christmas presents with as much excitement as we were opening those drums. Our new clothes and shoes were like heaven to us. We had to restrain ourselves to keep from eating too much. All the things we had talked about cooking when we got back to USA were nothing like this. It was hard to think about eating rice with worms again.

Most of the men wanted to go out of the brick kiln, but not me. The Japanese were going up the side of a mountain west of us with guns and equipment. We thought that they might not do what the Emperor told them to do and might come down on us for revenge. I thought it best not to let my guard down. In fact, I told myself that this thing would not be over until I set foot on the good old USA. Then I might relax a bit. There had been too many promises broken in the last four years to trust anyone.

OUR CAPTAIN AND HIS lieutenant had started acting as if they were the commanding chiefs and could tell everyone else what to do. The captain told us he had secret orders from General MacArthur that as soon as the bombing stopped, he was to take charge. These two appointed several of their favorites to higher ranks and gave them orders to go around telling everyone that close order drill would start and that all of us had to fall out at 7 a.m. Of all the things we had just gotten over with the Japanese, you would have thought that we could at least have had a little time to rest without being told what to do. After all, most of the men had lost respect for the captain and lieutenant long before now.

The days slowly passed between August 15th and the day we were told the surrender would be signed, September 2, 1945.

There was a movement to leave the camp on September 3rd and ride the train to meet the Americans in Tokyo. We would take all the men and get the sick out of there as quickly as possible in order to get medical help before it was too late for the patients. Everyone was ready to go when the men who had been put in charge by the captain came around telling us that the captain was not going to let us leave. We figured he was too scared to go and that he had come to us with this phony tale that he had secret orders from General MacArthur.

My standing army orders were clear. If you were captured you should return to your unit as quickly as possible. Some of us questioned the captain. All he said was, if anyone left without his approval they would face a court martial when they returned to the States. He also said he had every man's service number. I knew he did not have mine because since I had been captured, no one had been given my service number, most certainly not him. The lieutenant tried to boss everyone around, too, but we were not in the mood to listen to either one of them.

Each man was expected to take care of himself, clean his bunk, and help with preparing the food, if needed, and help the sick. But none of us wanted any part of fixing up the dump we lived in to impress the Japanese. We considered we had done that long enough. After four years of war and slave labor there was a limit as to what we'd take.

The Japanese were leaving us alone. Some of the men went into the town, but not me.

By the morning of the 3rd of September, a total of twenty-one of us were ready to leave. I went to see Ralph, Roger, Mack and Clyde. Mack said he was going for sure. Roger and Ralph said they thought they would wait to be liberated. When I asked Clyde what he was going to do, he said, "You saved me once, and you are not going without me now."

The early train came about 7:30 in the morning. When we started lining up, here came our captain's butcher men, telling us no one was allowed past the gate. So the twenty-one of us lined up and started towards the gate. A couple of guys up front had sticks. When some of the captain's guys stepped in front of us to stop us, we all yelled for them to get out of the way. We kept marching, pushing them aside.

The Japanese guard just outside the gate asked where we were going. The navy man that spoke a great deal of Japanese told him, "Tokyo." He stepped aside. We were all dressed in new khaki uniforms. As we walked to the train station, the captain and some of his newly-appointed henchmen were yelling for the Jap on duty at the train not to let us board. When we told the Jap we were on our way to Tokyo, he stepped aside, and we boarded the train.

The captain's men came to the train to try and pull us off. As they came to the train door, the train started. Those of us at the door just kicked them back. The Japanese men and women on the train were laughing and helping us yell at them. When we got down the track, we waved goodbye to them.

We all stayed close together. After three years we kind of knew how to handle ourselves with the Japanese. This was no time to be anything but polite and friendly. All went well, and most of us got a little sleep.

When the train arrived in the Nagoya Terminal, we were told how to catch the train to Tokyo. My thoughts were going back and forth about what was happening. It was hard to believe that we were on our way to try to meet the Americans, then get out of the country. All the time in the past three years in Japan, I could not visualize leaving Japan on a ship, but I could visualize leaving the Philippines on a ship; and because of that, at times I could feel that the time would come that I would be the one to give my life. I said a short, quick prayer for God to take care of me and the other twenty men. He had pulled me through so many tight spots, I felt He would do the same thing on this one.

As we boarded the other train, it was full of Japanese soldiers with very few women and children, and we felt less secure. Maybe these guys were coming in from a battle and would again take their anger out on us. Again, everyone of us knew that we had to stay quiet and keep a low profile. Soon a Jap sergeant came to us and told us to follow him. As we walked back several cars the Jap soldiers did not look at us in a very friendly way. We all spoke to some, but had no response from them.

As we approached the last car on the train we knew it was a special car. As we looked through the glass door we could see that the interior was red with gold trim. When we went in there was a Japanese general sitting at a desk in the very back of the car. He motioned for us to come on back and greeted us in English. He said he was the General in charge of China and was on his way to see General Togo. Also, he was the third-ranking general in the Japanese Army.

He asked where we were from and where we were going. When we told him we were going to General MacArthur's headquarters, he said that General MacArthur was in Okinawa, not Tokyo. He also said that when he and his troops got off the train, the American zone was the next stop. None of us would believe him, so we went on to downtown Tokyo.

The city was all burned out. Very few buildings were left standing. The B-29s had done their work. There were also no Americans in sight. We saw a streetcar not far away and we walked down to where it was, waited until the next one came, told the operator to put off all the people on it, that we were going to look for Americans. The other passengers were complaining, but he did it.

We took the streetcar all over the place, but could not find anyone who knew where the American troops were. After about two hours we saw a Jap army barracks so we got off, thanking the streetcar conductor. As we walked to the barracks, the guard came to attention and bowed to us. He thought we were operational troops. Our navy chief told him there was no need for him to bow because they had not done that for three years. A surprised look came on his face. He asked where we were from.

The chief told him we were POWs. He started begging us not to harm him. He had the gun, not us, but he yelled for the other Japanese troops in the building and about twenty-five came out. A first lieutenant was the ranking officer. They likewise asked us not to harm them. So the chief told them we wanted to go to the American zone and asked if they would take us, and the lieutenant agreed. So they all went inside, got their guns, and came out. We lined up in columns of two, then marched off to the train station with about twenty-five Jap soldiers around us. We had traveled about 500 miles with no one to defend us; now twenty-five Japs were protecting us from all harm!

When we arrived at the train station about two miles further on, the lieutenant got on one car and told all the Japanese already there to get off. They moved out. The train took us about ten miles and stopped. The lieutenant told us the next stop was an American zone and that they could not go in there. So we thanked them as they all lined up and bowed to us.

When we got off the train, we looked around the station but did not see any Americans. But in the street in front of us, many G.I. trucks were passing by. As we walked out of the station we saw one American. He was leaning up against a pole with a cigarette in his mouth. His gun was hanging down western style. We noticed an 11th Airborne patch on his shirt. When we asked where General MacArthur's headquarters were, he said, "Don't ask me." He told us that he had arrived at three a.m. that morning.

So we went to the street trying to stop a truck, with no luck. None of them would give us a ride. We walked to a small hill. Looking down the road we saw two G.I. trucks, one with the hood up. So we walked down to the trucks. A gray-haired master sergeant asked where our truck was. When we told him we did not have one, that we were POWs, he almost fainted.

We asked him where General MacArthur's headquarters were, and he pointed down toward the bay, "See that tall building? That's where the headquarters are." Then he asked how we were going to get there and we told him we guessed we would have to walk. "Well," he said, "Get in that truck, and I'll take you."

As we pulled up in front of the headquarters building we saw guards that were shoulder to shoulder around the place. An MP sergeant came out and we told him who we were. He said to wait right where we were. Soon he returned with a major. We were now in the hands of Americans. The feeling made my knees weak to think that at last we were back under American protection. What a feeling! As we approached the Grand Hotel, where General MacArthur's headquarters were located, we could see Old Glory flying in the breeze. I was saddened to think about the day back in Bataan in 1942 when we buried Old Glory with the intention someday to dig up the flag. It was hard to think how many men who had served died after the surrender of Bataan and never saw Old Glory fly again. But here I stood after all the things that had happened to us. Again a free man! What a blessing! Thank God!

The major had a lot of questions for us. One thing that all of us had to face, was the question of why all the men hadn't come with us. The major said he hoped none had died after we left and before the rest were liberated. If that had happened, he said, the captain might be in some trouble. We were asked to sign a statement saying that we made the trip without any trouble and that we did not have any guns or other devices to protect us. The major asked how many of us there were. A marine among us stepped out front, came to attention, shouting Japanese army orders, we dressed off and counted off in Japanese. Then he turned to the major and said, "All present and accounted for, Sir."

The major said "Take the men inside."

We were taken inside the Grand Hotel, where a crowd started gathering around us. They were giving us C rations. As we sat in a circle on the floor eating all we wanted, a lieutenant colonel came up to us and said he was General MacArthur's liaison officer. He told us that the general could not come and greet us in person, but that we were going home, that we did not have to do any work, and WELCOME BACK!

One of us spoke up, saying, "That's okay, nobody wanted to see him anyway." All the people in the crowd turned their heads to laugh. The colonel turned and left as fast as he could.

Soon the major came back and told us we had all checked out to be Americans, and he also welcomed us back. Soon we were taken to another building and given clothes and shoes, and were sprayed with some kind of chemical for bugs. After that we had a complete examination and were given three shots; then once more, our clothes were exchanged for new ones. I didn't care what they did now.

There was a hospital ship docked close by. Before we went for our final checkup, each of us was debriefed and asked about the Japs who beat us or were not good to us. This procedure was for the war crimes courts which were to take place later—and we also gave reports of any Americans who collaborated with the Japs and who caused us harm.

Then we went to a building next to the hospital ship in case we needed any immediate medical help. One of our group was looking up at the nurses on the ship and was waving, and not watching where he was going and walked into the back of a truck. His nose began to bleed. Another one was also looking up and was just one step away from walking off into the water. Mack grabbed him to keep him from falling in.

As we went into the building, a group of nurses and doctors waited to examine us. The nurse who was checking my heartbeat, temperature and blood pressure was holding my hand. She said, "Are you all right?

I said, "Yes; I'm free at last."

She said, "Your pulse is going faster than at first."

I looked at her and said, "Look, it's been about five years since I've seen an American woman, and you are holding my hand."

She jumped up, and told the doctor, "This man is ready for San Francisco!" None of us needed help from the hospital ship crew.

They took us out in the bay to a minesweeper ship for a good, navy-cooked meal. All the sailors were asking us questions. We received a welcome home from everyone. But when they put us in one of those beds, none of us could sleep. We were up and down all night. At 3 a.m. we were awakened, taken to eat a good breakfast, then on to the airport for a flight to Okinawa. We boarded a large cargo plane with no seats—we were strapped to the side next to the windows. As we took off, the valley below Tokyo was dark. To the northwest was Mount Fuji. The tip of its peak was white, illuminated by the rising sun. Below the white was an orange color, then the rest was black, the same as the valley. This brought back thoughts of the many times I could not imagine leaving Japan on a ship. Now here I was, leaving on an airplane. It was wonderful to look back and say goodbye to the Land of the Rising Sun and not be a guest of hell anymore.

As we flew over Okinawa Island, it looked as if every foot of land was covered with trucks, tanks, and equipment of all kinds. Ships covered the water around it and planes were flying in every direction. When we landed, a soldier was at the foot of the gangplank, welcoming us home. He knew we were POWs. I told the soldier that if they would give me enough of this equipment, I would go back to Japan and kill every one of the Japs.

To our surprise they put us on a B-24 with ten to each plane, and assigned us special places. My seat was the tail gun blister. The crew consisted of a pilot, copilot and navigator. They told us to look out for Jap planes, because a few had not given up yet. If we saw one, we were to yell out the location and they would give us the order to shoot if necessary.

The trip was uneventful. At one time the pilot and copilot were walking around the plane, and we asked who was flying the plane. They had two of the POWs sitting in the seats. We all yelled. Little did we know that the plane was flying on automatic pilot. At times the plane would sway from side to side, causing the tail blister to go round and round. They would laugh as I would yell out, "Will someone come and lock this thing in place?" The crew would then laugh some more.

When we arrived at Nichols Field in the Philippines, the captain was ordered to get into a pattern and wait for instructions to land. He yelled at the air traffic controller that his gas was too low to circle that long. As they talked back and forth, the captain said he was coming in. He said he did not care, he had to land.

As we went in low the plane hit the ground hard, bounced up above the buildings then came down hard again. As we rolled down the runway we were listing to the right. When we got off the plane we could see that the landing gear on the right side was bent. How close we had been to crashing!

We were taken to a barracks that was used to clear POWs who were in the Philippines when MacArthur had returned several months before. One of the first things I did was to go to Western Union and send a telegram to my folks. The major in Tokyo told us that our families would be notified that we were safe. So I sent a short message using my middle name, Dowling, so that they would know that I had sent it, that it was really from me.

The next morning I was asked to come to the orderly room. When I arrived, there was Nelda's brother, the one who gave me the hunting knife that I used to kill the Jap who tried to bayonet me at the Battle of the Points. He had been watching and waiting for me to return to the Philippines, if I was still alive. He hugged me. When I looked at him he had tears in his eyes. Very choked up, he said Nelda was killed in 1944 during an attack by the Japanese on their camp. He wanted me to put off going on to the USA and stay with them for a while and told me that I was welcome to be with them anytime.

Even though I was very saddened by the news about Nelda, I could not miss the chance to get on home as quickly as possible. He also asked me to come back to the islands to see them and to keep in touch through letters. He then gave me back the knife that he made me and that Nelda brought out of Bataan. The knife had Japanese blood on the leather of the handle. I was very glad to get it. As he left, he had trouble holding back the tears.

A typhoon was heading into the islands, so all planes going to the States were grounded. We had a choice. We could wait until the typhoon had come and gone or take a ship out within a couple of days. I talked to Clyde and Mack, and we decided on the ship, the troop transport *USS Pope*.

— 13 —

Return to the USA

AS WE CLIMBED ONTO the trucks that would take us to board the USS *Pope*, my thoughts were mixed about leaving the Philippines. I was very happy, but thinking about Howard Leachman, Turishky, Loucas, Engram, Sgt. Warren, Nelda, Vargas and so many others who had touched my life during this terrible ordeal made me sad. My mind was full of feeling for the Filipino people who lent a hand to me, and deep respect for many brave men who will never know what it meant to bring all this to an end. I knew I would always remember each of them.

There was a bond that would hold me to people who would not be able to share the happiness that I was sure was just ahead of me. So many times I've asked myself, "Why me?" How did Howard Leachman know that I would be the only one he knew who would experience this moment of freedom? It was like I had walked through a large, endless minefield with an angel guiding each step to keep me safe.

How different this trip to the pier was from the one three years earlier when we were loaded onto a Japanese freighter as slaves and shipped away to prison. When we arrived at the pier, I looked back towards the Old Walled City, the same as I had done when I arrived in 1941 with uncertain thoughts about the future. This time I wondered if I could handle being a free man again. Every step I took up that gangplank made me long to put the past behind me. Little did I know that this time in my life would be with me forever.

I noticed that truckloads of GIs were coming into the pier area to load. I was not sure how many troops this ship would take or who would be among them. Surely they were not all POWs. Soon I found out that most of these men had fought their way from Australia in some of the most bitter battles of the war. It made me proud to be sailing to the good old USA with such men. Their experiences were reflected in their tired and worn faces. Some were hard and cold inside. I understood from them that we were not the only ones who had walked through the gates of hell and were still there to tell about it. The ones who would talk a little sure knew what this trip home meant to them, the same way POWs knew. Most of them had been fighting since 1942.

As we sailed out of Manila Bay, to the right was Bataan, and to the left was Corregidor. Clyde had tears in his eyes the same as I did. I was not sure what he was thinking, but the bond between us was so close, we didn't have to say a word. Each of us knew how the other felt. We had a kind of empty feeling that was not easy to put into words.

WE WERE TOLD IT would take about sixteen days to reach San Francisco. The POWs did not have to do any duty, but most of us were looking for little things to do anyway. They had given us a small advance pay while we were in the Philippines. The first day they opened the ship PX, I bought a box of 24 Baby Ruth bars. Once I tasted the first one, I knew they would not last long. Before the night was over, I had eaten every one of them.

The ship's chief cook and I got to know each other pretty well. He asked me what food I missed the most. I told him potato salad and ice cream. He said he could not get me the salad but would give me ice cream and asked me to wait a minute. When he came back, he had one of the Navy pitchers full of ice cream, layers of each kind, with a big spoon.

I sat under a stairway eating. He came by a few times asking how I was doing. Before long when he came out, I handed him the pitcher. He looked in it and said, "Man, you ate it all, nearly a gallon." On the trip I ate all I could eat and still got up from the table hungry. I could feel the weight stacking up on me. When I left Japan I weighed 168 lbs. Now my pants were not easy to button, and my shirt was about to pop the buttons off. I would go up on the deck and try to do some exercises, but there was no stopping the weight gain.

Days passed slowly, and it seemed like a month before we approached the West Coast, but we finally got there. Every man aboard was getting excited about going under the Golden Gate Bridge into the San Francisco Bay. Back home, USA! We all talked about what we would do when the bridge came into view. To me it was as though I were arriving at the heavenly Golden Gates, not a bridge. I knew I had regained my freedom the day I walked into General MacArthur's headquarters in Japan, but that feeling was nothing like this. My heart was pounding, and I'm sure my pulse was beating faster than when the nurse held my hand in Japan.

The day was overcast with scattered clouds. Every spot on the deck was taken. I expected that when the bridge came into view it would be as if we were standing on that knoll in Japan when the first dive bombers came in to bomb the docks. We would all be jumping and yelling, like being at a good football game. Everyone was looking far ahead in hopes of being the first to see it.

All of a sudden a low voice said, "There it is, right ahead of us." As I looked up, I saw that we were only a short distance from the bridge. No one said a word. Everyone looked at the bridge in total silence for several minutes. Then all hell broke loose. It was a wonder someone was not knocked overboard. You could not stand still or keep from yelling. What a surprise for all of us. Home sweet home.

EVERY MAN ABOARD WAS getting his things together and trying to get ready to set foot on US soil. Some men who were quiet by nature and not usually talkers could not stop yelling. The USS *Pope* went straight to its designated pier with no delays. As we approached the pier, we saw Old Glory waving in the breeze high above it. What a sight. My legs were weak, and my breath came in gasps.

After order was restored, the POWs were the first to disembark. I was the second one to get off the ship. The man ahead of me was walking fast, but I stopped and got down on my knees and kissed the ground. He saw me, turned, and kneeling down beside me, did the same thing. After that most of the men followed suit.

There was a large crowd of people a short distance away wait-ing for their loved ones to arrive. They were waving and shouting, "Welcome home." Some were waving small American flags. What a feeling now to be walking on US soil—ground that so many times I thought I would never see again. It was hard to believe, and a feel-ing of unreality pervaded everything. It was just about impossible to think it was happening!

They loaded us into busses. As we were loading, all of us were hugging each other. The joy we shared together was one of love and understanding that I will never forget, realizing how much we meant to each other. No one was there to greet us, but this did not surprise me. I guess none of our families knew we were coming. We knew, though, that we had each other to share this time with.

From the pier, we were taken to Letterman General Hospital to be checked out. We were assigned to a building some distance from the main hospital, along with a nurse and a few helpers. As we walked into the building we saw real beds made up nice and clean, one for each of us. No straw mats. The beds were even up off the floor for a change. And no body lice in sight.

As I walked over to pick out a bed, I noticed a pitcher of water on a side table along with a few little tidbits to eat. This simple gesture of thoughtfulness was, again, hard to believe. About 8 p.m. a new nurse, a very young one, came on duty. This was her first day of duty after getting out of school. She told us bed check was 9 p.m. and that everyone must be in bed at that time. Just before the lights were turned off she came in to see if all of us were there and to tell us that if we needed anything during the night, to come to her station. She said we must all be quiet and considerate of others.

About thirty minutes after the lights were off, most of us were having trouble sleeping in a soft bed. Soon some were on the floor with pillows and a blanket. The restroom was full, each one saying he could not sleep. A few went outside and crawled under the building. The young nurse heard something that made her come back through the building. When she saw most of the beds empty, she was alarmed and turned on the lights trying to get the men on the floor back into their beds. She also tried to get everyone out of the restroom.

When she counted the men, there were still some missing. She went back to her station and called someone to report several missing men. When the head nurse got there, the young nurse was crying and said she could not handle men who would not obey her orders.

The head nurse asked us where the other men had gone. We took her around to the back of the building where the missing men were sleeping very well. The head nurse turned and said, "Okay men, sleep wherever you want to." Most got on the floor. It took about five days before we were able to sleep comfortably on clean, fancy beds.

I had sent $10 per month to the Bank of America before I left in 1941, and when Clyde and I got a pass to go into the city, we went to the bank and picked up my money. That night we went to Playland Beach, a park with roller coasters and lots of other rides. He and I met two girls we took on the roller coaster. Since we had had a few beers, we rode about three times. After the ride, Clyde and I went to a restaurant, and the waitress presented us with a bill for two dollars. The waitress was very pretty, and when I gave her a $20 dollar bill Clyde looked at her and said, "Just keep the change, Sweetie." He gave away my money!

A COUPLE OF DAYS later we were told we could make one long distance phone call and talk as long as we wanted to at government expense. It was time for me to call home and let the family know that I was alive and well in San Francisco. I was wondering what they would say and whether they would be angry with me, so I wasn't sure just how to handle myself. After all, I did leave without telling them for three months where I was. Now nearly five years later I wondered how they felt and if they held it against me for getting caught and being a POW, like Tokyo Rose had said they would.

My mother answered the phone. When I told her who it was, the phone went dead. I waited, then my aunt answered by saying, "Who is this?"

I answered, using my middle name, Dowling. The phone went dead again. I waited, and soon my oldest sister answered the phone. When she asked who it was and I told her, the phone went dead again.

I was still waiting when my Dad came to the phone, asking in an angry voice, "Who is this?"

I said, "Dowling."

He said, "I knew you were not dead." He then told me, "I think I have three women on my hands, though, who look like they are dead."

He went and got a pitcher of water and poured some in each of their faces. When he came back to the telephone, he said, "It looks like they are still in the land of the living."

Dad asked where I was and dozens of other questions. He also told me about telegrams they had gotten from the army. The first one told them I was missing in action. Two and a half months later they got a second telegram telling them that the army had no word that I was alive, so assumed that I was dead. Then several months before I got home, an army representative came to see them with my dog tags, saying that my remains were found in the mass grave at Camp O'Donnell, the burial site where I had thrown them in 1942.

The army tried to pay them $10,000 to settle my life insurance claim. My Dad asked if he would have to repay the money if I were later found alive. The representative said that, in that case, the army would request repayment. So my Dad told them just to keep the money. He had a feeling that I was still alive. He also told them that if anyone could make it, his son could. Dad also told me that my brother Rupert was in the service somewhere close to Japan, that my brother O'Vaughn was still in Europe and that they expected him home anytime.

My oldest sister wanted to know if I was in bad shape and how long I would be at Letterman Hospital. If I would be there for a while, she said, some of the family would come to see me. They all expressed joy and thanks that I was alive. I was beginning to feel much better.

ONE DAY WE WERE lounging around on the grass outside the hospital when a train brought five railroad cars into the area. The engine unhooked itself from the cars it was pulling and left them on the tracks. Soon a crew came to unload the cars, which contained supplies for the hospital. When noon came they closed the car doors and left for lunch.

The six of us watching looked at each other with the same thought: the tracks curved around a small hill, and we could have some fun by moving the cars around the hill, where they would be out of sight. So we unhooked the last car and got behind it with a technique we had learned in Japan. One by one, we moved them all out of sight. When the crew came back to unload the cars the sergeant in charge got on his phone reporting that the train had come back and moved the cars out. He requested that someone call the railroad and tell them to bring them back. When they checked with the railroad they were told that the train had not come back and moved anything.

"Well, five cars didn't vanish into thin air," the sergeant said.

Soon a major arrived. No one thought to go around the hill to see if the cars were there. All that time we were watching, laughing to ourselves. Soon the major looked up at us and asked how long we had been there.

"You see where or how the cars were moved?

"Yes," we told him, "they are around the turn in the tracks."

The sergeant took off and then came back to report back that they were indeed where we said they were.

When the major asked us who had moved the cars, we could not keep from laughing. "This is a serious matter," he blustered. "If you guys know anything you must tell me."

We confessed and told him that we had moved them.

"You guys?" he said, with a surprised look on his face. "How did you do that?"

We told him we learned as POWs in Japan how to move railroad cars.

199

He thought for a minute. "Well," he said, "would you guys go and move them back?"

So all of us plus all of them went down the tracks; we were to perform the miracle and they would watch us do it. We put our shoulders against the first car and started pushing, using the Japanese words for push, "*Hey, no gosha!*" over and over again. As we gradually speeded up the pushes, the cars started to move. Thee guys watching could not believe their eyes. It took a little while, but we got the cars back in place. The major told us he thought what we had done was a very bad joke, but that since we were POWs, he would let the matter drop.

EVERYONE AT LETTERMAN GENERAL Hospital was good to us. They had treated so many of the POWs from the Philippines they knew just what we needed. We were told that we would be transferred back east soon. In the meantime we were all enjoying our new freedom.

The psychological counseling we got was basic and hardheaded. The doctor whose job it was to "repatriate" us was a no-nonsense kind of guy. His feeling was that if you could walk and talk, you were ready to face the world like a normal person. We had about twenty minutes of being told things like, "Everywhere you go to eat they will furnish knives, spoons, and forks. All restrooms have toilet paper. When asking for food to be passed to you, ask politely. Please pass the beans. Or please pass whatever." After that bit of advice, he told us, "Now go out and act normal."

We would soon have a chance to try out our skills at acting normal. After seven days of treatment, we learned that the twenty-one of us would fly back east with a stop at the Phoenix, Arizona Air Force Base, and at Dallas, New Orleans, and Thomasville, Georgia. They would fly each one of us as close as possible to his home.

When we flew over the Rocky Mountains in our DC-3, the plane had to get up to around 15,000 feet. It was cold, and the cabin was not pressurized. Then when we dropped down to the Arizona desert, it was like an oven.

When we landed at Phoenix they told us we were to be guests of honor at a dance and would sit at the base commander's table. That afternoon Clyde and I took a walk down the street from the barracks where we were to spend the night. When we passed this small building, a lady came out asking if we were with the POW group. She said she thought we were because of the uniforms we had on and asked us to come in. While we were talking, the two nurses who were on our plane came walking by. I went out to say hello and asked if they would be at the dance. They said they were not invited to the commander's dance, so we invited them to come in with us.

The lady who ran the little recreation unit had called two other girls, asking them to come down to see us. Soon three other girls showed up, and we were offered some drinks and beer. There was a jukebox, and someone suggested that we dance. When the music started, Clyde and I danced with a different girl each time. We paid no attention to time and neither did any of them. When closing time came at 10 p.m., we were surprised to know it was that late.

The nurses started to leave. We asked them when we boarded the plane the next morning if they would call us sweet names to make the others jealous, and they agreed. When we walked into the barracks all the guys asked where we had been and told us that we had missed the commander's dance, where we were supposed to be. All the MPs were looking for us and for the commander's daughter. Apparently, they thought we had done something to her.

The sergeant in charge of the barracks called the MPs. When they arrived they wanted to know if we had seen the missing daughter. We told them where we had been and that the two nurses and three girls who lived on the base were with us at the recreational building. Calls were made to the commander's home and also to the lady who invited us into the building. Within thirty minutes it was all cleared up as far as the MPs were concerned, but the other nineteen POWs were ready to beat us up. They were at the dance with a couple of thousand airmen and 200 girls. We had had five of them all to ourselves.

The next morning as we boarded the plane, the nurses called Clyde and me "Darling" and kissed us on the cheeks. Boy, did that get the guys going again. The nurses made comments about how close we all were to each other.

AS WE MADE OUR WAY toward our first drop off in Dallas, I felt a little sad about leaving the others after all we had been through together. After Dallas, it was New Orleans. That's where Mack and Clyde would get off. Clyde was as close to me as anyone had ever been. We hugged goodbye with a promise to see each other later.

Now there were only six of us to go to Thomasville, Georgia, to a small Army hospital there 200 miles from my home. When I called home, my sister said some of the family would come to see me. They asked many questions about my health. At that point I was gaining weight fast, but still had a bad limp from the old bayonet wound. Outside of that problem, my health was as good as anyone could expect.

I was wondering about my girlfriend. None of the family knew anything about what had happened between us before I joined the Army in 1941, but I was pretty sure she was not waiting. At least I felt that way.

My sister told me that my brother O'Vaughn was in Europe, but that they had not heard a word from him since the war in Europe ended. They were becoming afraid something had happened to him at the war's end and could not find out anything from the Army. We would just have to wait for news.

When we asked the doctor how long we would be in Thomasville, he told us maybe a couple of weeks. When he said that, I told him I wanted to go home right away. He replied that I couldn't because they had my clothes locked up. I looked him in the face and said he might have my clothes, but I had on these pajamas and I would go in them.

He told me that if I wanted to go that bad he would see what he could do. The next morning when he made his rounds, he told me I could leave the next day on a 45-day leave, and I was in high spirits. When I called my sister to let her know I was coming, she told me excitedly that her phone had rung a few minutes earlier and the operator had said there was a collect call from Georgia. She thought it was me, but when she answered and called out my name, "Dowling," the voice on the other end of the line said, "No, this is O'Vaughn. Why did you say Dowling?"

"Well," she said, "he is alive and is in Thomasville, Georgia."

Not only had she found out O'Vaughn was alive, but in the same telephone call O'Vaughn found out that I was still alive.

— 14 —

The Last Leg of a Long Journey

WHEN I WAS TOLD I could go home on a 45-day leave, it was like a dream come true, but a dream not without some apprehension.

Now I would be able to face some of the problems left unresolved for five years. I felt that there would probably be a lot of hurt feelings between my family and me. I knew I had changed in every way. From what I could see, the whole United States had also changed. What World War II had done to all of us was hard for me to understand. Leaving like I did in 1941 without telling anyone, I might find my family could not understand who I had become, and likewise, I might not understand them. I knew it would be hard for me to step back into a way of life that was normal in 1941.

I also wondered if my girlfriend was still around and whether or not she had gotten married. How would we even know each other, with the experiences we had shared so long ago being the basis for our former feelings for each other?

Now that I was free, I found myself wondering if I could even accept the concept of freedom. Could I become a normal person again? No one would ever know how three and a half years as a slave in a prison camp changed everything about me. Sometimes I considered not even going back home, for I knew the adjustment would be very difficult to make, if it could be made at all.

I already missed the close friendship of fellow POWs. They had become such an integral part of me that I knew this closeness would never go away. When you have someone who will lay down his life for you through a bond that is as close as your own blood, it's hard to say goodbye to that person. You realize you will no longer have them and their understanding to lean on. I knew how they felt and they knew how I felt, but no other person in the world, except the ones who had been there as POWs, would ever understand, because they have had no experience even remotely comparable to it.

It kept running through my mind that we had been told by Tokyo Rose during her radio broadcasts how our country looked upon us as cowards and did not want us back. If that turned out to be true, I did not know how I could handle it. I just knew God had gotten me through a difficult time and I had faith that He would help me now. I would surely need Him.

GETTING HOME MEANT A bus ride of several hours. When the doctor gave us our release to go on leave, I made a call to my cousin who lived closer to the hospital than my actual home. I asked him if he could take me the rest of the way home if I rode the bus to his hometown. He said he would be happy to do so. I also felt he could tell me what kind of reception I might expect when I got there.

It was so good to see him. I was amazed at his excitement about my being home after so long. The welcome he gave me made me feel much better. He had been told that the ones going through what I did might be reluctant to talk about their experiences, and he was very careful about the questions he asked. I told him anything he wanted to know that I did not mind talking about. He and I were as close as cousins could be back in our school days, but again, he, too, had grown and changed while I was gone.

When we arrived home everyone ran out of the house grabbing and hugging me. To my surprise, my brother O'Vaughn was there from Europe. He had arrived just a few hours before I got there. My mother, father, oldest sister Sarah Nell, Betty Carolyn, my youngest sister, Mabel, O'Vaughn's wife, and his daughter, Vonciel, were all there.

All my questions as to whether or not I would be welcomed evaporated. The love that was expressed was beyond anything I could have imagined. Tears of joy were on most everyone's face. My oldest sister had a time controlling herself. She showed the love she had always expressed to me, plus much more. Vonciel was excited to have her dad there, someone she only knew from a picture since she was born.

My father had changed the least of anyone. With his sense of humor, he showed me that he was proud that I was back and was safe. My oldest sister Sarah Nell was beside herself. She and I were always close, and she could not stop hugging me. My mother had suffered so much worrying about me. It was like she was in a daze, maybe so surprised because she had almost accepted the fact that I was dead. My youngest sister was really excited and told me how sorry she was that before I went into the army she got me so many spankings from my mother by saying I hit her when I didn't.

Later, when my oldest brother Waverly came with his family, he said it was hard to believe that I was home safe. He too had almost accepted the fact that I was dead. His wife, Margaret, who was a school teacher, was very glad to see me home, but had a few words of remonstrance, like "You should never have gone in the first place."

Waverly and Margaret's first child, Johnny, said he thought I was never going to get back. When the war started he was recovering from an operation. He had a radio in bed with him and all of a sudden he started crying. When asked what was wrong, he said the Japanese had bombed the Philippine Islands and that's where Uncle Dowling was stationed.

Their oldest daughter, Sarah Glenn, was small but looked at me as if to ask, "Who are you to be causing so much fuss?" Thelma, their youngest child at the time, was a pretty little girl, but didn't understand all of what was going on with these Army guys.

THE NEWS THAT BOTH O'Vaughn and I had gotten home at the same time had caused a stir in our small town. We came into the house and closed the doors. People who passed the house were blowing their horns, and the phone kept ringing with people giving their "best wishes" and "welcome homes" to both of us.

Soon, my mother and the other women prepared a big dinner for us. I said earlier in this book that if I could have just one more meal with my family, the Japs could execute me and I would die in peace. Now my wish was coming true. I was sitting down at the table with my family eating the meal I had dreamed about so many times and that I doubted would ever come to pass.

Between O'Vaughn and me, the war stories were going strong, along with the stories about what the folks at home had to put up with, like the rationing of tires, gas, sugar, meat, stockings and many other things that were in very short supply.

My father had a humorous story to tell about getting tire ration coupons at the courthouse. Then Sarah Nell told about two young boys coming to her house selling magazines. Supposedly the money made was going for War Bonds. When she told them that she didn't believe she wanted any, they started ridiculing her, telling her that she was not a true American, had no interest in helping our boys overseas, and that she didn't understand what the war was all about. She then told them that she had one brother in a POW camp somewhere in the Far East and another brother in Europe who had been in the drive from Africa to Italy and beyond. Another brother was in the U.S. Navy in the Far East waiting for the invasion of Japan. So, they had better get out of there before she called the police. She had heard on the news that some people were in the area selling magazines and that they had no connection with the U.S. bond program.

My little sister Betty told about our dog named Tan. He was a good family pet. I did not know he would miss me so much, but being the youngest boy, I guess I spent more time with him than anyone. Betty said that after the war started, Tan started howling at night. As he would howl, Mother would start to cry. The louder he howled, the more Mother would cry. Betty would go out and bring Tan inside to stop him from howling.

After dinner my mother said she had a surprise for O'Vaughn and me. She left the room. When she returned she had several packages and put them on the coffee table. "Here are your Christmas gifts for each Christmas you missed," she told us. Then she added, "Wait. I have something else."

When she returned to the living room she was carrying the mirror from the hallway wall at the farmhouse. Two hats were hanging on it. One was the hat that I had hung there when I rode off on the motorcycle, and the other one was O'Vaughn's that he had hung there the day he left for the army. When my family moved from the farm to town, mother had put the mirror on her lap and said that no one was to take those two hats off. They were to be taken off when the boys returned home, never dreaming that we would return together on the same day. Leaving the hats there after they got word I was dead was their way of keeping a ray of hope for both of us surviving the war. Since my father had a feeling that I was still alive, there was hope that some way I had made it. Now here I was, taking the hat off to find many moth holes in it. I kept that hat until the house burned in 1949.

Our celebration that night went on into the early hours of morning. There was so much to catch up on with both of us and with the rest of the family, we just couldn't bear to go to bed. It was early morning before we finally got any rest.

The next day O'Vaughn and I wanted to go up the street about half a block to Raymond Davis' store, not only to get a coke, but to visit with them. When we got to the curb of the street, cars started stopping with the passengers talking to us and welcoming us home. Someone went to get us a coke. The cars kept coming by until 4 p.m., when we were able to get back to the house. Then phone calls followed. That Sunday we went to the Methodist Church, where everyone extended overwhelming love to us and welcomed us back home.

Almost everyone wanted to talk about what had happened in the POW camps. I felt as if the folks were so interested, I would be glad to talk to them. Before long I had over a hundred invitations to come to dinner and talk about my experiences. I think it did me some good to talk everything out. I was eating everything in sight, still getting up from the table feeling hungry and like I needed more to eat. My appetite stayed that way until the weather got warm in the spring.

The next thing I wanted to know was whether or not my girlfriend was still in town and whether she had gotten married. When I made a call to a fellow classmate to ask about her, he said she waited for me for over three years. When word came that I was dead, she had started her life over again. He said, "I hate to tell you this, but she is getting married this coming Sunday."

My heart dropped, though I did not blame her for not waiting for me. The only time I saw her again was about two months after she was married, when I wished her the best of luck. She said, "I'm very sorry. Please do not blame me."

As I looked at her I still felt close to her, and it took me a while to get over my feelings for her. Maybe it was all for the best, but so many times the hope that she had waited for me was one of the things that made me push myself to keep going and not to give up. While in the slave labor camps of Japan, at times when my system was so low that I could not remember the names of some of my family, I could still remember her and how I had felt when she got on the train that morning of July 3, 1941. That feeling never left me the entire time I was away from home.

My brother Rupert was supposed to be in the Far East, but I had no idea exactly where or any confirmation that he was really there. He was unable to be with us. After some special training at the U.S. Naval Station, Bainbridge, Maryland, he headed to the South Pacific as a member of a military government team. Rupert joined the First Marine Division in February, 1945, on the island of Pavuvu, located in the Russell Islands, a part of the Solomon Islands.

The mission of a military government team was to follow the invading forces into cleared enemy territory and locate and take care of the civilian population. The team would round up women, children and the elderly, account for them, feed them and treat their medical needs. Rupert did not know until his ship left Pavuvu that his destination was Okinawa, the largest of the Ryukyu Islands, just 90 miles from Japan.

On April 1, 1945, U.S. forces landed on Okinawa. The next day the military government team went ashore. This battle was one of the fiercest of the Pacific during World War II and there were many civilians to look after.

Then, word came that Iheya Shima, a small island northwest of

Okinawa, had considerable Japanese forces thereon and an invasion was planned for May, 1945. This invasion required a government military team, and Rupert was selected as a member. As it turned out, the weather was terrible and after several postponements, Iheya Shima was invaded with little resistance. Once again, there were many civilians needing the help of the government team.

Rupert had been on Iheya Shima from May until August, 1945, when the atomic bomb struck Hiroshima and Nagasaki, bringing the war with Japan to a close. The last two Kamikazi planes to leave Japan landed on Iheya Shima without damage to our forces.

Rupert knew that I was a prisoner of war in Japan, and that I had been sent to Japan earlier from the Philippines. As soon as word was received that the war was over and the treaty was signed, Rupert received permission from his commanding officer to go to Okinawa to see if he could find out anything about the prisoners. He stayed on Okinawa for about a week and a half, finding nothing. At the request of his commanding officer, Rupert returned to Iheya Shima. Later Rupert heard that I had been on Okinawa at the same time he was, on my way home, but he had not been able to locate me. I, of course, had no idea that Rupert was even in that part of the world, or was even a member of the armed forces. Based on the point system for returning to the United States, Rupert did not return until March, 1946. Amazingly, there were three brothers from our family in World War II who came safely home. How lucky we all were.

DURING THE TIME I was home for my leave, I was notified that the Thomasville Army Hospital was closing and that I should report back to Moore General Hospital in NC at the end of my 45 days. My younger sister Betty was lining up dates for me. She had about fifteen ladies ready to go out with me, but I felt I must first get over my feelings of having lost the girl I had loved so much. It wouldn't have meant much to me to date someone at that point. A date should be fun, a time to become better acquainted, and a time to lay a foundation for a friendship or maybe a more involved relationship later.

When I reported to Moore General Army Hospital, the other five men who came back across the USA with me were there too. They all had joyful stories and tales of wonderful reunions with their families.

Fortunately, we were assigned a location in the hospital where we could be together. Everyone was very good to us. It was now time to go through all the examinations to see if we were fit to stay in the army. We were told that the army was in the process of downsizing, but any one of us could stay in because we were regular Army before the war.

My desire was to get a release from the hospital so I could make a choice, not just be given a medical discharge. If I had the option when I was discharged from the hospital, I could either go back to active duty or get a regular discharge. My thinking was that if I had trouble making it outside the Army I could always re-enlist.

When the men I was with went to Asheville on a pass, we would all stay together. We were easy to spot as ex-POWs by the patches on our uniforms. Many times we were stopped and asked questions about our time as POWs.

Once when returning to the hospital, we ran into a guy at the bus station we knew from the prison camp. He had once said that even if he was a POW, if he ever heard the word *grourr!* (the word the guards used to summon one of us) when he got out, he would kill the person who had said it.

He was not in the hospital, but at the bus station standing in line to get a ticket. We hid behind the line of seats and yelled *grourr* at him.

He quickly turned around, but could see no one. He thought he was hearing things. After he was back in line we repeated the yell. This time he jumped out of line, took out his pocketknife, opened the blade, and started looking around the bus station for the villain who was about to be his kill.

Then he got close and saw us, and said, "Well, I will have to kill all six of you because I do not know who did the yelling." After all of us hugged him, he settled down. He went back to the ticket counter asking when the next bus would leave Asheville. The ticket agent said in 30 minutes a bus would leave for New York City and another bus would leave for Miami, Florida. He told us he would take the bus to Florida to get away from these guys because he wanted nothing to do with any ex-POWs. Then he told us he was just traveling around seeing the country and did not care where he was going.

I did not know that Moore General Hospital had a section of the hospital for guys who had mental disorders. When I got my release from the hospital my orders were to report to Ft. McPherson in Atlanta, Georgia, where I was to decide if I wanted to stay in the service or get a discharge.

When I walked up to the discharge counter, I was asked by a T-5 if I wanted a discharge. I told him yes. He asked on what terms. I answered, "Points." You were credited with certain points for where you served, for how long and certain other criteria. It took from 70 to 80 points to get a discharge.

He handed me a blank pad and said, "Well, Sergeant, sit over there and figure up your points." I told him, "I do not know what you get points for."

He looked a little surprised, and said, "You do not know how to figure your points? How do you know you can get out?" At that point he looked down at the envelope holding my orders. When he saw the return address as Moore General Hospital, he said, "Just stay there a minute." Then he walked over to the officer in charge and said, "Captain, I think we have another nut from Moore General Hospital."

The captain said, "I'll take care of it." When the captain walked up he said, "Sergeant, I understand that you wish to get a discharge, but you do not know how many points you have and do not know how to figure them."

I said, "That's right, Captain." He said, "Where have you been?" I told him I'd been overseas all during the war and spent three and a half years as a POW. He asked me, "Why didn't you tell the T-5 that?" I replied that the T-5 had not asked me.

When the Captain figured my points, I had a few less than 300. The captain tried to get me to sign up for another three-year hitch, but all I wanted was *out*. Within a short time I had that regular honorable discharge. As I passed through the main gate on my way outside, I said goodbye to the army, but I did sign up for army reserves.

After getting my discharge I returned to my hometown with hopes of leading a normal life. The men who controlled the political strings there wanted me to run for mayor. That was the first job they had planned for me, but I wanted nothing to do with it. I did not know for sure what I wanted, but it sure was not a job where I had to do what everyone told me to do, because I had been doing that for the past five years. I wanted to be free to do what I wanted to do for a change, and enjoy the new freedom that the discharge paper gave.

IT WAS GREAT BEING home, but everything that had happened to me was still roiling around inside me. It was like two people came home. One of them was the boy I had been and the one my family saw when they hugged me and talked to me. The other was the man I had become, full of memories and feelings that I could not deal with. Things had happened so fast, and I had not been able to overcome the fear, the suffering, and the rage and pure hatred that I had inside me. When the war with Japan ended on September 2, 1945, I was a Japanese prisoner of war in a slave labor camp on the western coast of Japan about 500 miles by rail from Tokyo.

That was just a few weeks ago. Now I was supposed to try to adjust to a life that for four years I thought I would never live again. To my family and friends I was plain old Glenn Dowling Frazier, the soldier that was home again. But I knew I was no longer that person. My thoughts were often full, not of the freedom and love that surround-ed me, but of the Bataan Death March, of the times that my body was so badly beaten and sick that I feared I would not live another night.

Now I could see my family and friends, enjoy freedom and not have to wake up every couple of hours to check and see that things were all right. I could realize that I was still one of the living, and sleep-ing without the threat of a Jap guard's rifle butt slammed against my head. I did not have to look forward to a small bowl of wormy rice or hear the sounds of Jap guards screaming at a fellow POW who was only trying to go to the slit trench to relieve himself. Maybe I would be able to take a bath at least once a week and not every six months in cold salt water.

I was tormented by questions while coming home. How would I be able to sleep without body lice crawling up and down my body? Sleeping without the lice after three and one half years would make me feel all alone. I could not imagine having lots of covers to keep me warm enough to keep the circulation going in my toes and fingers, or not sleeping with others and all of us piled up like pigs in a pigpen to get warm. Just being able to walk into a barbershop and get a hair-cut, without dull scissors pulling the hair out of your head, was unbelievable. Being able to purchase a clean undershirt or a pair of shoes, without cutting holes in them for my toes to stick out would be wonderful. And, how would I be able to handle not having to ask permission to go to the slit trench or to the bathroom?

No more would I have to guard my spoon so I would have a way to eat the watery rice. No more would I have to shake the one next to me in the morning to see if he had made it through the night. Even just to conceive the fact that I might not be beaten or killed today seemed like a dream.

All of these things had been so real for me every moment for so long. Then we knew that the Jap guards had standing orders, the minute an invasion took place on the mainland, to shoot all the POWs. We had accepted this fate long before now. The only thing we had to look forward to was the feeling that the Japs would get what they deserved, that their defeat would serve as a lesson to all evil governments that waging war against others and treating their prisoners as though they were animals, like the Japanese did, would not go unpunished.

Now I was told we were going home. There were many thoughts and questions in my mind, "I was going home; the nightmare was over! Could I live with freedom after all of this? Could I adjust from the horrors of war and the brutal treatment received while I was a POW? Could I lay down my guard and walk with pride? Could I hide the feelings that suddenly took possession of me?

Thoughts of my fallen buddies who were not able to come back brought tears to my eyes. Their mothers, dads, sisters and brothers would wait patiently at the pier hoping to see their loved ones coming down the gangplank and running into their arms. They might wait for months, going back to each arriving ship to wait for their family member to return and never see him get off any ship. They would be wondering if he were dead and where his body lay on foreign soil.

How long would it take me to really feel free again? Free to choose where I wanted to go and free to do what I wanted to do. The return to my hometown was such a wonderful experience. But soon my mind would go back to the past. I would remember when the slightest noise would find me sitting straight up in bed looking for the Jap guard who might have shot or hit a POW. Instead of my subconscious mind working to adjust to being free and safe, it kept returning to what had been a way of life in the past. It was hard to wake up and know where I was and realize my life was not on the line. Every morning I would have to convince myself that I was home safe.

SOMETIME AFTER I RETURNED home, the nightmares started, and for many hard years they became a constant part of my life. It was easy to justify drinking until I passed out. I could drink my dark thoughts away.

When I was in the hospital in San Francisco, I was told by the doctor that all I had to do was "go out and act normal" and all would be fine. It was hard to keep that advice in mind when my dreams were as real to me as when I was actually living these horrible times. I would awake feeling as though there were lice running all over my body. I would jump up and turn the lights on to examine my clothes because the feeling was so real.

My nightmares were not something I could talk about to just anyone, since people would surely think I was crazy. It would be a complete waste of time to even tell anyone about them except another person who had experienced being a POW. Night after night, I would struggle with the problem of readjusting. Each morning when I woke up, I was as tired as though I were back in the prison camp. While these dreams were going on it was like having a real life experience again, then waking up and trying to go back to sleep without getting back into the same battle for my life.

How could I answer the simple question I was asked time and time again, "Are you enjoying being home?" Could I tell them it was really hell, and that my honest answer should be, "No, I am not." So my mind would send mixed signals. I did not know how to answer such a question.

After being trained to fight the war and having to kill to save my life and those of others around me, I got to the point that I believed I had become a killer. On Bataan I would lie in wait for a chance to kill a Japanese soldier. I was proud to be able to kill another of the enemy, and that became my way of life. When a day passed and I missed a chance to kill another one of them, I felt like I had failed to do a good job that day.

When I came back home to a small, quiet town where shooting a rabbit might be the biggest thing to happen in a day, it was impossible for me to live a normal life. The nightmares nearly every night brought back another life experience so vividly that it felt real, not allowing me to separate my present life from what had happened to me while I was gone. This was a time where I could see a fine line between killing and not killing. My thoughts would bring me to a point of thinking that maybe to kill someone would make things easier. I would think that I needed to kill to satisfy a hidden urge within me and to get that monkey off my back. Maybe if I had been able to kill a few Japanese soldiers after my prison camp experience and then returned home, it might have helped.

It was impossible to discuss this urge with anyone. It was an everyday fight to keep these thoughts out of my head, and I knew of no place to get help. Then I would face going to bed each night, knowing that I was going to dream about the Japs again, hiding under bridges, running, jumping off embankments into the water, hiding under cars, being shot at with no way to defend myself.

The horrors of the war were with me every day and night for the next twenty-nine to thirty years. At times I wished I had never come home. I imagined how peaceful it would be to lie down in a quiet place and find the peace that only comes with death.

Now that I have told my story so many times on television, spoken about my experience to many individuals and family members, and made personal appearances to many types of groups telling them about my past, I have finally been able to reconcile myself to a more normal life than the one I spent as a POW. I will never be completely free of my memories, or my nightmares, but I am *free!*

I have chosen the path of my life in my later years, and I am using my years spent in misery and pain to let every person who will listen understand the completely helpless feeling of not being able to make even the smallest decision on your own behalf and how it feels to be totally without control of your own health and well being. Think about the simple choices you make every day. When you brush your teeth you choose the time, the make of the brush and the brand of toothpaste. All choices are important, but the choice of freedom is the most important choice for every person and especially every American.

Apathy is the greatest danger to Freedom. My years as a POW will not have been in vain if in hearing and reading my story others will realize how important it is to be free. We must preserve our country and ourselves from the danger of being controlled by persons who want to deprive us of the greatest of all gifts—*our right to decide everything for ourselves!*

— 15 —

The Rest of My Story

AMERICA HAD CHANGED SO much during the war that it took a while to get adjusted to the new order of things. My relationships with everyone that I had known before were different now. In fact, some of my closest friends were quite distant to me for some reason I did not fully understand. Other friends had moved away to work in factories to support the war effort. Women were holding down jobs that had only been held by men before the war. The women also seemed to have a much more independent outlook and were most certainly not as friendly as they were before the beginning of the war. I realized that I had a lot of catching up to do.

Not long after my return, a good friend who had a Plymouth and Dodge car dealership offered me a job. Selling cars was easy in those first days after the war. Everyone had had to patch up their old ones to keep them going for the past five years. Now there was a waiting list of the people who wanted to buy a new car, and, thanks to the factory jobs that had opened up during the war, they had money to pay for them. Color, style—none of these things mattered. Someone was ready with a handful of cash to drive our new cars away.

It didn't take me long, however, to realize that selling cars was not what I wanted to do for the rest of my life. The trucking business in those days was interesting to me. Transporting goods by truck offered a great opportunity because the war was over and America was starting to expand. The railroads were losing business because trucks could pick up and deliver door to door, saving a lot of money in handling charges.

I decided to go with a small trucking line that hauled freight between Mobile and Montgomery. I could call on businesses and increase shipments for delivery to, from, and between all the towns along Highway 31. This kind of sales offered much more opportunity to me, and I took advantage of a newfound ability to "sell and close the deal."

Things were going well. By now I had found a girl that I wanted to marry. She said yes, and in June 1946, we were married and moved to Mobile, Alabama. But even after I married the great stress of trying to adjust to any kind of normal life was still with me, and so were my nightmares. Every night I would suddenly awaken, sit up in bed and check all around me to see that everything was okay, the same as I had done for years while in POW camps. At first my wife had compassion about my fears and tried to handle the nightmares and help me handle them. But as time went on, instead of lessening their power over me, the dreams became more and more real. In them, I felt like I had returned to the actual times I had spent as a POW. I also developed a deep hatred towards the Japanese. I would wake up from my dreams yelling and swinging my arms, trying to defend myself against the ghosts of my past.

Soon my wife could not stand to sleep in the same room with me. She already knew some of the background of what I had been trained to do and had done in the Philippine Islands. She felt her life was in danger when I reacted defensively to the nightmares.

We decided that I needed help from the Veterans' Administration. The first thing they did was have me go to a psychiatrist for evaluation.

In those days, that was like sticking a "crazy" label on me. I knew for sure that I could not tell anyone, not even my own family, that I was seeing a psychiatrist. My psychological problems also made it very hard to get a job.

As time went on, my wife could not stand the strain of my troubles. She felt frustrated and helpless in her efforts to help me resolve them, and after seven years we were finally divorced.

It was hard for me to work for anyone else, so I started looking for a business that I could own and be my own boss. Because the trucking industry was growing and was an exciting young, new industry, I felt it offered me a great opportunity. A good friend in the moving and storage business talked me into buying a half interest in a company in Shreveport, Louisiana, where I could work as owner and manager. Since I was a veteran and a POW, I had an extra edge in getting transport contracts with U.S. military bases.

As I settled into the job of building my new business, I decided to take advantage of my G.I. Bill of Rights to attend college and enrolled in the Meadows-Draughn Business College for a Bachelor of Science degree in business administration. I also took courses in accounting. While I was attending classes, the college began offering the courses in the Elmer Wheeler Sales Institutes. After taking the course myself, I was asked to teach the course, which I did for a couple of years.

When problems with my partner in the moving and storage business began, I sold out my share and went to work with Grey Van Lines out of Chicago, becoming one of the top salesmen in the nation.

When the Korean War began, I tried to get back into the army. However, due to my VA record of psychiatric treatment and the general state of my health at that time, I was not able to do so. Then, out of the blue, Howard Van Lines of Dallas, Texas, called me and offered me the position of National Sales Manager. This position required me to move to Washington, D.C. where I became very successful in building up the company. In a short time we were up to 300 agents and had added 30 company offices. I was very busy training all the sales force and lobbying for the moving companies in Washington D.C.

At the end of my sixth year with Howard Van Lines, the business had grown from one million in annual sales to over sixteen million. When the owners decided to cash out and sell the business, I went to work with Greyhound Car Rental in Washington DC. This job was all right for a while, but I had a strong urge to get back into business for myself.

In 1958 I moved to Charlotte, North Carolina, and worked a franchise location for National Car Rental. My business soon expanded to South Carolina. But all was not well with me. Due to poor health and the resulting inability to provide personal management of the business, I sold out the car rental business.

The same problems that I experienced during my first marriage were responsible for the ending of another marriage. My bitterness against the Japanese for their treatment of me and the other POWs had fostered a burning, almost irrational, hatred for them that was consuming my mind and my entire body. This black passion affected my thinking and reasoning in everything I did.

The nightmares that had followed me all these years made me a nervous wreck. I could barely digest my food. I felt as though I was strapped in and held in bondage with no say over my body or my actions. It was like being in the camps again. There was little help I could get from the VA because they didn't know much about the lasting effects the war and years of being under such physical and mental strain had on the former prisoners of war.

For several years after I sold the car rental business, I drifted from job to job. I spent over a year with a Holiday Inn advertising contractor traveling all over the country. Then I went to Tampa, Florida and bought a hundred small motorcycles and rented them to riders. I sold that business and went back to Atlanta, where I started a business called Delta Car Rental. The partners I had there were very difficult to work with, so I severed my relations with them and moved to Denver, Colorado, where I became interested in the development that was taking place in the mountains with tourism and new ski trails and lodges. I became involved with the Park Meadows Corporation, which built small condos in Aspen, Breckenridge, Vail, Winter Park and Steamboat Springs, Colorado.

After this experience, I decided once again to go into business on my own. I went to Kansas City, Missouri, and organized a company by the name of Glenco Development Company. I purchased 630 acres of land around the Lake of the Ozarks. I then opened an office in Denver and contracted to purchase 1500 acres between Aspen and Colorado Springs. My intentions were to build a chain of condos in various areas for skiing around a huge hunting lodge in Wyoming. I also planned to build in Florida, close to Disney World. I traded for the Cumberline House in Nassau, Bahamas, envisioning a vacation exchange program for condo owners.

Things were going well until the National Land Use Law was passed, and the formation of HUD made it impossible to sell your way into a development. In addition, it was expensive to obtain the necessary permits for building. With all of these adverse conditions, the money for development dried up. Also, in the 1970s, the false gas shortage occurred, and it was hard to get people interested in anything that was farther than a day's drive away from their homes.

I began selling off different parcels of land. I reduced my holdings until I was down to the 630 acres on the Lake of the Ozarks and free and clear of debt. In 1972 I was listed in Who's Who in the West because of my vision on the vacation exchange program and the progress I had made in developing the properties I owned. During a time that should have brought a feeling of great success and happiness over my achievements, my life was still mixed up because of my hatred for the Japanese. *I just could not get over this hatred.*

The 630 acres I still owned in 1972 was pledged to a bank for a loan to develop it in the amount of one million dollars, but in order to get this loan I had to make my banker a partner. Then in 1977 the bank president was shot to death. The bank was in financial trouble and the FDIC moved in and closed it. Because I had the banker as a partner, after an 18-month legal battle, the FDIC stepped in and took everything I owned, even the house I had built on the Lake of the Ozarks. The bank then re-opened with new management.

I moved to Atlanta for a year and then went to New Orleans, where I opened a gift shop in a motel. There I met a gentleman who had a great invention, and I decided to invest in it. The money I had saved went into building a prototype. I got a contract to manufacture and sell the product throughout the entire world. Just as the invention was ready to go into production, the inventor dropped dead from a heart attack. All the papers in his lock box proved to be worthless, and I could not find any engineers who could make it work.

During the winter of 1981, I began to experience severe pain in my chest. I went into the Veterans' Hospital at Iowa City with pneumonia. In doing x-rays to determine the extent of the pneumonia, the doctors found a tumor in my right lung, resulting in a surgery that cost me half of that lung.

While recovering in the Intensive Care Unit from the operation, I promised God that if He would give me one more chance, I would do better. Eight months later the cancer came back. I refused chemo treatment and instead used a treatment that I obtained from members of an Indian tribe. Within sixty days of beginning this treatment, all the cancer was gone.

I moved west again, first to the Panhandle of Texas working with the farmers trying to develop a way to pump water for their crops at a lower cost. Everything we tried failed to operate the big well pumps that were used to irrigate the large circles where they had corn, wheat, or other crops planted. I moved farther west, this time to Arizona, where I formed a trust for the purpose of helping gold miners finance the operations of their small mines. At the time there were no banks or any individual who would make loans to gold mining operations.

After four months, I went to California in hopes of finding private investors to finance the mining. Due to California laws that made it hard to use escrow companies, I moved to Las Vegas, Nevada, where I could put assets into an escrow account. I made several attempts to get investors to buy the equipment to process the ore. It was hard to find trustworthy personnel to perform this process because as soon as they saw real gold coming out of the ore, they went off on their own, leaving my operations without qualified personnel. It became a very complex problem, and as a result I sold out my interest, hoping to find a less stressful business operation.

After moving from Las Vegas to Florida, the church became more important to me than it had ever been. Here, people were friendlier and I began to go to church regularly and to engage in Bible study.

WHILE LIVING IN THE western desert area my problems with the nightmares kept me from getting proper sleep, which made it hard to keep going. My feelings against the Japanese had grown until every time I saw an American driving one of their cars, a flare of anger flashed through my entire body. Everything in my life was being affected by these feelings. At times I would resort to drinking to try to forget my problem. It became impossible to tell anyone that my experiences in a war over 30 years ago were still haunting me. My body was telling me that something had to be done to end my problem, but when thoughts of resolving it came into my mind, I found it so strongly embedded in my beliefs that it was impossible to do anything about it. I was reaching the end of my rope.

Early one morning, about 2 a.m., I awoke from sleep, and before I really knew what was happening, I was kneeling by my bed praying to God. It was like an uncontrollable force working inside me, even giving me the words to say. In that prayer, I asked God to help me shake the curse that was controlling me.

I had asked my preacher at times about ways to get help and solve my problem, only to be told that I must forgive the Japanese. I said, "Oh no, I can't do that. They have never apologized to all of us, how can I do that?" And I continued to suffer.

But the force within me this night brought the tears. I cried my eyes out. Every thought that passed through my mind was like a voice inside me saying, "You must forgive everyone and everything that has hurt you. You must forgive the Japanese and forgive yourself for harboring this hate for so long."

These thoughts made me realize that the Japanese did not even know I was in the world, and here I was killing myself over my hatred for them. I asked God for help. He told me that every time thoughts about this hatred for the Japanese came into my mind, I should reject the thoughts, give them to God, and never take them back. I must *refuse* to take them back every single time the hatred tried to return. I must pray every day for God's guidance. I must follow the passage in the book of Matthew 18:21-25 for help and understanding.

Then Peter said, "Lord, how often am I to forgive my brother if he goes on wronging me? As many as seven times?" Jesus replied, "I do not say seven times; I say seventy times seven."

Following these guidelines was the hardest thing I ever had to do. It took a couple of years to finally cleanse my heart and body and find release from the pain I had inflicted upon myself with my own thoughts. The mind is very powerful. It can be an enemy to your body and to your health. God's healing begins in the mind and can bring both peace and healing from old wounds and the acid bitterness that can destroy a life.

As I worked through my problems using the guidelines I had been given, I started sleeping better. My attitude became more outgoing towards others. My tolerance toward others and their actions was greater. I became more aware of my past feelings and what they had done to me. I could see that some of my friends who went through the same experiences as I did died early in life.

Before this experience in prayer my health was not good. My diet was a disaster, so I had to start building up my body by changing what I ate plus taking food supplements such as vitamins and minerals. The things I liked most to eat were not good for me, so some eating habits had to be broken.

With all these positive changes, my health improved. I no longer had the terrible nightmares. My attitude became positive, not negative. I even went to a Honda dealership and sat in a Honda car. I told my pastor that he could call the news and tell them that I was at the Honda dealership kissing a Honda car. The flares of hate no longer burned when I thought about the Japanese.

As I studied the word in Matthew, it became clear what had happened to me. The changes within me now became a blessing. I no longer felt the bondage that had controlled me for so many years. I was becoming free and able to enjoy what I could now call a totally new way of life.

With the help of several friends, I began to get back my life. I had lost a lot of things that most people take for granted. Now I had the ability to live a completely free life—free from all hate and free from bad habits. Once again was I living a life filled with good things and the happiness this life brought.

Being able to make these changes was not easy. It took almost two years for me to see for myself what the changes were doing to my once worn-out body and exhausted mind. My health took a turn for the better. I was able to enter and stay in a loving relationship with a woman who shares my new hopes and dreams.

Now I knew. The past can be remembered, but it does not have to be relived. To know God's peace is the freedom within which we can accomplish our desires. Thank God, my heart is now free to love God and all His other creatures. How grateful I am that I discovered the way out of the bondage of hatred and the inability to forgive.

I will never go back.

Epilogue

IN 1990, I returned to the Gulf Coast where I had planned to retire. I went to the National Guard to see if I could serve again. They sent me to the Alabama State Defense Force that is under the Adjent General and part of the home front and National Guard. After reviewing my records and the Field Commission of 1st Lieutenant in the Philippine Army in 1941, they gave me a Captain's rating. Over the years of good attendance records I was presented the rank of a Captain, then Major, than Lt. Colonel. After completing the required time in rank, I was promoted to the rank of Full Bird Colonel. I am still active today and plan to remain active for several more years, that is, as long as I am needed.

www.HellsGuest.com

usafirst2008@yahoo.com